YOUTH SERVICE
AND
INTERPROFESSIONAL
STUDIES

edited by

INGA BULMAN
MAURICE CRAFT
FRED MILSON

PERGAMON PRESS

OXFORD   NEW YORK
TORONTO   SYDNEY   BRAUNSCHWEIG

Pergamon Press Ltd., Headington Hill Hall, Oxford

Pergamon Press Inc., Maxwell House, Fairview Park, Elmsford,
New York 10523

Pergamon of Canada Ltd., 207 Queen's Quay West, Toronto 1

Pergamon Press (Aust.) Pty. Ltd., 19a Boundary Street,
Rushcutters Bay, N.S.W. 2011, Australia

Vieweg & Sohn GmbH, Burgplatz 1, Braunschweig

First edition 1970

Library of Congress Catalog Card No. 74–124060.

C

834937

Printed in Great Britain by A. Wheaton & Co., Exeter

08 015736 X

0080157736X

YOUTH SERVICE
AND
INTERPROFESSIONAL STUDIES

Contents

Introduction

BETWEEN 1958 and 1961, a series of conferences at the Universities of Keele, Leicester and Nottingham brought together lecturers in colleges of education, social workers, clinical and educational psychologists and nurses to consider the common ground in their respective courses of professional training. Subsequently, a national Interprofessional Committee was set up to examine the issues in more detail, and this has given rise to a number of regional study groups in interprofessional development. In Chapter 11 of this book, Professor J. W. Tibble discusses the deliberations of these early meetings, and assesses the possible implications for the future training of teachers, youth leaders, and other members of the "helping professions". These events are among the sources of the "interprofessional" idea.

Westhill College of Education in Birmingham trains teachers, and its courses include options in youth work and social work. It is also one of the six agencies offering training for full-time youth leaders, and closely allied with this is a course for community centre wardens. A further department of the college trains students, mainly from overseas, who return to work in their own countries as teachers, youth leaders or social workers. This interprofessional background lies behind the conference mounted by the college in 1967, and at which the papers presented in this book were given. With Westhill's special interest in Youth Service, the discussion of interprofessional development has been centred on this theme and this is not, perhaps, an inappropriate starting point for such discussion. As Frank Dawtry, (Chapter 6), Lesley Sewell, (Chapter 8), Dame Eileen Younghusband, (Chapter 9), and other contributors point out, Youth Service stands between the world of education and that of social work. Administratively it belongs largely to the one, but in terms of skills it leans increasingly towards the other. The youth worker's professional role, it seems, is both creative and ameliorative. A. N. Fairbairn's discussion of the advent of the teacher/youth leader in Chapter 4, similarly illustrates the professional no-man's land occupied by Youth Service. But it is in the belief that this ambiguity gives Youth Service *a key role* in interprofessional development that these papers are presented to a wider public.

These are clearly early days in the development of interprofessional training, but as Maurice Craft suggests in Chapter 10, the possibilities have been discussed for at least a generation; and at a time of change and of rapid expansion in teacher education, the training of youth leaders and most branches of social work, and at a time, also, when the structure and organization of welfare provision is undergoing careful reappraisal, there may be a strong case on purely practical grounds for a rationalization on interprofessional lines. The overlapping professional viewpoints and clientele, the common areas of study and of technical skill, all indicate the economy and efficiency which might result from such a rationalization. For the most part there are common sources of recruitment; and there might be great gains in flexibility and in collaboration in the field (as Fred Milson argues in Chapter 2) if specialization followed a common core course, and allowed for easier transfer from one role to another at a later stage. As Chief Inspector R. D. Salter Davies suggests in Chapter 5, an alternative means of achieving this greater flexibility might be through the provision of carefully graded ("sandwich") in-service training.

In the papers which follow, many of these issues are discussed. But specialization of role may reflect specialization of need and not merely historical accident, and this too is considered. Herbert Heginbotham, for example, in Chapter 7, argues that the roles of youth leader and youth employment officer are complementary but distinctive; and many members of the welfare professions have a legitimate concern that interprofessional development should not produce a "hybrid" qualification and a *less* functional pattern of specialization. At another level, there are also the many practical difficulties to be considered—varying admission requirements on entry to training, and the consequent variation in duration of courses; the several Ministries and the numerous training bodies involved; the established separatist traditions, and so on.

Finally, *Youth Service and Interprofessional Studies* attempts to blend the findings both of theory and of experienced practitioners. In *Part One*, Professor Mays' overview of adolescence, followed by Fred Milson's discussion of the young immigrant and by Professor Marsh's survey of the social and administrative context of Youth Service set the scene with a broadly theoretical view. *Part Two* considers a number of the practical issues raised by interprofessionalism, taking Youth Service as the theme. *Part Three* looks more closely at Youth Service, social work and teaching from the viewpoints of both theory and practice, before examining the interprofessional idea in a little more detail.

The book is not presented as any kind of original contribution to interprofessional thinking, but merely as a contribution to the continuing debate. The editors venture to hope that it will encourage further speculation and experiment and that it will be quickly outdated by substantial advances in interprofessional theorising and interprofessional development.

[EDITORS' FOOTNOTE: These papers were put together in the autumn of 1967.]

PART ONE

THE ADMINISTRATIVE AND SOCIAL CONTEXT

This section outlines some significant aspects of the context in which the discussion of interprofessional development takes place. It begins with a broad overview of the changing place of young people in our society; and this is followed by a consideration of the special problems of the young immigrant, and by a review of relevant issues in contemporary social policy and welfare provision as a whole.

CHAPTER 1

Young People in Contemporary British Society

JOHN BARRON MAYS

WE LIVE in an age when every aspect of private and public life is exposed to general scrutiny. Our culture grows increasingly narcissistic and inward-looking almost to the point of producing a kind of social hypochondria. We are very conscious of time and its passing and are so bemused that even the ages of individuals are regarded as everyday news items.

It is not surprising, therefore, that in a period like ours, concern about youth should not only be openly manifest but should also at times take on the proportions and appearance of an obsessional neurosis—a neurosis, moreover, shared by young and older people alike: the young being obsessed with their own youthfulness and their elders being obsessed by the alleged problems they are said to create.

The topic of youth has hence taken on an almost excruciating emotional overtone today. One can hardly bear to hear the term "teenager" invoked for fear of the inanities which will surely follow such an invocation. I have heard adolescence described as a kind of illness. I have heard it said that youth must be led by youth and will respond to no other age group. I am also old enough to remember the motto of the Hitler Youth Movement, "Youth shapes its own destiny", and once again in the manipulated political activities of the Red Guards in China we see the emergence of a similar menace to the safety of the entire world. In youth we see imaged powerfully the two greatest psychological and biological

3

forces which, by their very universality and vitality, present civilized man with his most baffling problems; namely, sexuality and aggression.

This is, of course, to see youth in a world-wide context more or less unrelated to the empirical realities of specific societies. But it is perhaps advisable to remind ourselves of two main points before going on to say more about young people in Britain today. These are first, that it is unrealistic special pleading to talk about adolescents as though they lived in a social vacuum; and, second, that youth always has a functional role to play in any kind of society which itself has any claim to be regarded as healthy. I will have more to say on this topic at the end of my paper but it is necessary to bear both these points in mind when discussing concrete contemporary situations in terms of intergenerational stress. Youth is not so much an unavoidable as a necessary stage in human social development, and more particularly is functionally hyperactive in a rapidly changing, technologically sophisticated and pluralistic society such as ours.

It is legitimate, therefore, to speak of both physiological and of sociological adolescence. The former is related to the latter in so far as it brings it into being in the first place, but the two concepts are far from being identical and must be kept carefully apart in any analysis. The fact of physiological maturity coming where it does, in the early teens, complicates what I have called social adolescence and makes it more frustrating an experience than it need be in simple biological terms. There can be no doubt that the current trend which makes for a prolongation of adolescent dependency is well nigh irreversible. What Dr. Wall[1] has referred to as "a social and academic apprenticeship" seems both unavoidable and likely to become even more prolonged in the future, as the demands for more and more skill are advanced and as the clamour for more certificates and degrees as occupational passports and status symbols influences more and more groups with any kind of professional aspiration.

Not only is an ever longer dependency period likely for young people as a result of rising status desires and technical demands, but there is also reason to believe that this tendency also arises from an ever-growing tenderness on the part of older people towards children in general. This can be documented in a number of ways but if a high-water mark of this attitude exists it is surely in the abortive government white paper *The Child, the Family and the Young Offender*, issued in 1963, which got into some terrible contortions in an attempt to produce the right procedures to cope with the various age-groups its authors proposed. The failure of the white paper derives from the fact that its authors failed or refused to accept (I do not know which) the idea of earlier maturation. And by maturation, in this context, I am not thinking about the alleged, but to my mind as yet unproven, claim that biological maturity is being reached at a progressively earlier age, but that what we may call psychological maturity (i.e. readiness to make one's own decisions and to assume the burden of responsibility for living one's own life), is certainly attained by a great many young people by their late teens. If by that age they can drive a car (one of the most lethal weapons in common use), surely they can be allowed to put a cross on an election paper or marry the boy or girl of their choice without mummy's or daddy's permission.

If one could propose a formula for individual responsibility it would run something like this:

$$\frac{\text{permitted autonomy}}{\text{desired autonomy}} = \text{responsible individuality.}$$

If we are going to get the answer to that problem right we have got to make sure that both top and bottom lines are appropriately scored so that they cancel out to make a unity.

Social problems, then, so far as adolescents are concerned, are the result of various obstacles arising, either in the structure of society or in their own psychology, which prevent or hinder the development of all-round maturity. They should only arise when something somewhere has gone wrong and if, as many would argue, adolescence is almost always a period of stress, strain and conflict, the reasons for this will, in my judgement, be found more in the quality of social relationships than in the nature of the adolescent development phase as such. Nor do I believe that the theory that older men are sexually jealous of the rising generation can account for more than a small minority of over-critical and frustrating adults. What I am saying, in effect, is that we should be able to handle the difficulties that arise quite naturally and normally even in our rather complicated modern industrial communities. We should not expect intergenerational hostility, jealousy and conflict to flare up into such proportions that anything like alienation becomes discernible. I do not accept the view, therefore, which some psychiatrists have put forward in such terms that the adolescent's need is to be in revolt against society and/or against his parents. It is not that I deny the evidence that revolts of this nature occur: what I deny is their inevitability or the associated idea that we should be prepared to accept such a state of affairs as normal and healthy.

I do not want to be misunderstood here. I am not implying that I am in favour of a tame and meekly conformist youth. Of course, youth must challenge the ideas and scrutinize the values of his inherited social world. I agree with Tawney, who said long ago that "the first duty of youth is not to avoid mistakes, but to show initiative and take responsibility, to make a tradition, not to perpetuate one". But there is all the difference in the world between a critical review and a creative reappraisal of our ethos and institutions, and an almost wholesale rejection of every part of the established order and a stubborn refusal ever to accept compromise or to support policies based on gradual evolutionary advances.

But enough of preambles. In a paper of this length one is driven into making generalizations or as some of my friends less kindly term them, sweeping statements. Anyone who is a parent or who as a teacher or youth leader comes regularly into contact with young people knows that they are all different and that their dissimilarities straddle the frontiers of sex and social class. At the same time, they have many similarities and it is these which especially interest the sociologist who is on the look-out for regularities and patterned behaviour. We must stress similarities in order to generalize and we must generalize in order to make sociologically significant statements, none of which need be true for any single individual.

A great number of books and research publications have recently appeared on both sides of the Atlantic dealing with both general and more specific aspects of youth in contemporary society; many of them are first rate, most are important. But it is impossible in a brief lecture to do justice to their variety and I have appended a list which will enable interested readers to pursue the subject in greater depth. Meanwhile, at the risk of over-simplification and the charge of superficiality, I want to put before you a modest typology of young people, derived, in the main, from the analysis of this literature but based also, to some extent, on my own observation and experience. I do not claim that this typology is complete but perhaps it can form the basis for an orderly discussion of the subject which, unless we are careful, can often ramify into a whole series of side-tracks and blind alleys to produce ultimate confusion and intellectual despair.

Group 1. This group comprises those youngsters who react with hostility against frustrating environmental circumstances. They may during their life histories, have been denied the love and care and control necessary at some crucial phase of their development, but they are also, quite clearly, products of our inadequate educational system which has signally failed to fit them for rewarding and respected jobs. They are denigrated by the social system, made to feel inferior at every stage of their development, and allotted a position at or near the base of the social pile. In the old days they were condemned to dead-end jobs or to long periods of unemployment: nowadays their lot is less cruel in purely financial terms, but in terms of the status hierarchy and the values and goals which are enshrined in our predominantly bourgeois culture they are failures and misfits. The plight of these young people cut off from the mainstream of society has been tellingly described for us by Havighurst and his colleagues in their study of River City,[2] a midwestern American town of 45,000, made in the late 1950's. Havighurst estimated that something like 29 per cent of the age group were made up of drifters and the socially alienated, coming "from all the social classes" although "the lower-middle class seems to furnish more than its proportional share of them. They are the elements making for instability and disunity in the society." We do not know what proportion of young people in British society today could be so described, but, even though their numbers were by comparison with the North American situation quite small, we have reason to believe that they do exist and that their presence is a badge of shame to us all to the extent that we do not care sufficiently about their unhappy condition.

Group 2. This group is made up of youngsters who are similarly socially depressed and unsuccessful but who do not react to their frustration and denigration by open hostility and aggression against respectable law-abiding sections of the community. They avoid violence yet are not retreatist, content themselves with taking part in minor infringements of the norms and petty illegalities and associated rackets. The type is admirably portrayed by William Foote Whyte in his classic study, *Street Corner Society.*[3] Within their own subcultural milieu they are reasonably content and adequately adjusted.

Group 3. This group consists of the more thoughtful and intellectual and morally committed young people irrespective of social class background. They are the latterday Angry Young Men: anti-establishment, anti-apartheid and anti-nuclear war. They take part in public demonstrations and invariably adopt a radical and humanitarian stance. But they are not merely anti-this or that. They stand positively for the ideals of brotherhood, freedom and co-operation, especially between the youth of all nations. Many of the student activists of whom we hear much these days belong to this group of questing and questioning young people.

Group 4. This is a smaller and deviant section of the youthful population who reject the contemporary world and along with it almost everything else. It is difficult to believe that their attitudes are based on reason or informed by idealism; rather they seem to be inherently nihilistic, trying to escape from the responsibilities of life via drugs and alcohol and unrealistic other-worldly philosophies and cults. Some are sexually promiscuous, repudiating all moral codes. They live on the margins of society, on the shadowy fringe of social life, withdrawn amongst their own kind, living in derelict buildings and even in caves, a modern type of youthful hobo. How far this group continues the original beatnik posture and how far it is merely a self-conscious and rather unwashed sort of bohemianism is difficult to gauge. But for all their claims of independence they are clearly parasitic. As one ex-public schoolboy turned beatnik is reported to have said: "You may ask how we live in the winter, man. I tell you: we don't know how. We just do. We ponce on others, we live from day to day, that's what."[4]

Group 5. These are the new men and women of the affluent society, for the most part working class or lower middle class in origin but viewing the world around them confidently and even a little pugnaciously. They do skilled work, enjoy a high standard of living and are well satisfied with themselves. They enjoy the physical and sensuous good things of life—cars, clothes, money, holidays, sex. They do not feel inferior to other social groups and classes; in many ways, in spite of their brashness, they are warm, likeable types cast in the Arthur Seaton[5] mould.

Group 6. This is made up of those middle-class, grammar, and public-school battalions who have made a good adjustment to their own favourable background and who have sufficient ability to get on well in the milieux of professional, business and commercial life. They have passed the necessary examinations, gone through the hoops and judged by normal standards, are making a success of their lives. Some are the Jackson and Marsden upward mobiles, others have been born into white collar and professional families. In a sense they epitomize those values which our contemporary society seems most keen to promote and reward.

When I advanced a similar typology to this in a book published some 2 years ago,[6] one reviewer pointed to an omission which I must now make good. He complained that I seemed to have forgotten about that body of young people who are less able than the average, who are almost by definition lower class but who are well adjusted to their station in life and accept their lowly status with equanimity—the contented proletarian base, in fact, who have no urge to rebel. To some extent these youngsters are in my Group 2, but I am willing to concede his point that there is a group of un-ambitious and unfrustrated people in the bottom ranks of the secondary modern schools who will never make social trouble and whose attitude is characterized by passive acceptance of inferiority. I do not know how many of them they may be at any one time but I most devoutly hope that their numbers are diminishing as educational and occupational opportunities become more extensive. It is, I think, a group we could well do without.

Of course, there is obviously a great deal of overlapping between my hypothetical groups and many individuals will not fall neatly into any of my categories. Perhaps the majority of young people today—in British society anyway—will be found in Groups 5 and 6, while Groups 1, 3 and 4 make up those whom conventional society regards as deviants and problems. It is these latter groups who receive so much of the publicity and who have given a pejorative flavour to the term "teenager". Most, if not all, healthy youngsters go through a bohemian phase during their development, like to dress a little flamboyantly and demonstrate their individuality, but this must not be mistaken for either social deviance, psychological abnormality or permanent rejection of the conventional world. I do not want to sound patronizing here, it is so easy to slip into a patronizing attitude, but a touch of rebelliousness and a degree of unconventionality is desirable not merely in youth but throughout life. The moment we find ourselves ceasing to protest we can be sure we are spiritually dead.

So far I have said very little, if anything, about what is sometimes called teenage culture and teenage society—something which is obviously a fairly recent and novel social phenomenon and one which has attracted a great deal of attention from many different quarters. I have been taken to task elsewhere for failing to see the significance of beat groups and pop culture and what some people consider to be an exciting new network of communication connecting the younger generation of all classes and income groups. Peter Laurie, for example, in his most interesting essay *Teenage Revolution*[7] talks about "a most important change" since the mid-fifties. Since then, he declares, "the teenagers have come into nationwide contact with each other. They have formed a society of their own." He sees clothes, songs, motorbikes, etc., as channels of communication for a new society of youth held together by dance and clothes' styles and the possession of guitars and transistor radios. "In Liverpool", he states, "this change was sudden and startling. The new beat music imported by Bill Haley and his Comets in 1955 dissolved away the old violence-oriented gangs and replaced it by beat groups and their devoted followers".[7]

In 1955 I was living in the centre of Liverpool, in the heart of dockland not very far from Ringo's birthplace, and I am certain that this is quite untrue. Untrue not because Bill Haley's Comets did not evoke a sudden and lively response in the way of skiffle and other groups at that time. This most certainly happened and it took some of us by surprise—a very pleasant surprise, may I say—to see such genuine spontaneity amongst city youngsters. No, the statement is untrue because of its reference to the alleged violent gangs for, in my judgement, few if any such gangs had existed in Liverpool for a very long time. I do not know *as a matter of fact* if they ever existed.

I think that it is easy to be misled by superficial impressions into believing that a revolution has taken place as a result of the insurgence of adolescent pop culture in the past 10 years or so. Commercial interests have fastened upon it and battened upon it and in the process stifled most of the spontaneity. The whole thing has become glaringly contrived, and youth, like so much else in our society, has become a kind of human merchandise. I do not deny that young people pre-eminently exhibit an important trend in modern society, i.e. the investment of much of their personal and emotional life in leisure-time activities. Industrialization and affluence have made this possible for us all and it may well be true that young people today to an ever increasing extent are deriving their values from the world of leisure and recreation with the falling away of some of the older values and beliefs—almost *faute de mieux*. At the best, however, I think it is only true to see pop youth culture as a kind of massive escapism. The image of the golden lad who makes good overnight, the backstreet girl who achieves sudden stardom, is not very different for most of us from the older idea of winning the pools or the even hoarier idea of breaking the bank at Monte Carlo.

Youth may seek meaning in leisure but I doubt if they will ever find it there!

Pop youth culture is, I think, a gigantic red herring drawn across our trail by those people who very much dislike the established social order and who most passionately want to see someone rebelling against it. So they tend to see rebellion in every shred of youth culture, even when it is not there and even when it has clearly become in its turn a new kind of conformity as intolerant of difference as any other group movement. The reason for this is twofold: first, the commercial and financial institutions of our society are enormously tough and resilient and in the end pull everything within their orbit, and, second, you can never found a creative revolution merely upon a rejection of "ingrained orthodoxy" and "stuffy convention". You need something much more positive and idealistic than group narcissism to found a new way of living. Youth, of course, possesses by definition what a new way of living demands—namely idealism and energy—but do not, for God's sake, let us deceive ourselves into believing that the Mods and Rockers who used to flutter the seaside weekends in Southern England a little time ago, or the cavorting of the Monkees or any other group under whatever outlandish name, or even the vitality of Carnaby Street or the advent of the mini-skirt is a national release of creative activity which will eventually transform our whole western way of life. It seems to me, on the contrary, that the Stones and the Mods and all the others are themselves youthful out-croppings of the very values of the society which some people think they are going to overthrow! They represent, that is to say, the exploitation of spontaneity and the industrialization of leisure.

Perhaps I had better return now to my six or seven groups and see whether any special problems arise or whether all is well with them. Without being over-judgemental or obsessionally concerned with social pathology, it is possible to identify a number of problems which are worth considering further. There is, first of all, the very real and I should have thought undeniable problem of the privileged on the one hand and the underprivileged on the other. Differences of birth, natural endowment and opportunity still divide us into two nations or rather two cultures and life-styles. The barriers between the two cultures are permeable and so chronic frustrations are avoided, but there still remains the basic problem of achieving social justice and of giving to each generation equal chances of growth and self-development, most especially, of course, in the educational sphere. Until these difficulties (which are, in my view, both moral and technical) are overcome, we will almost certainly be faced with a proportion of youngsters who are rebelling against the futility of the life they are being offered. And with some justification!

Allied to this major and general social problem, in which youth is unavoidably immersed, is one which arises from the fact that children are differentially endowed. The failures who see themselves justly underdogs may not cause very much trouble, or, rather, some of them may not feel the temptation to react negatively and hostilely against their fate. But there is another aspect to this. What about the successful ones? What about those who are intellectually so endowed and emotionally so bland that they fit snugly into the system and do well by it? What about Jackson and Marsden's[8] unvaliant eighty-eight, in other words, the ones who rose from the ranks and came to look down on the "dim ones" who had been left behind? Godfrey Smith once remarked,"The hunger march may be over but the rat race is on".[9] All this matters very much for the condition of our democratic society and for the quality of life which we transmit to future generations.

Critics and social observers have commented on two major problems amongst young people which may or may not be more noticeable nowadays than heretofore. Amongst youth itself they point out a tendency to over-conformity and tameness, on the one hand, and of under-conformity and destructiveness on the other. Both attitudes are deemed undesirable but for very different reasons. The ultra-tame conformers are certainly not the stuff of which empire-builders or national heroes are made. Empire-builders and national heroes may be out of date. They may be positively danger-ous people to have around in any great numbers. However you judge that issue, I think that such a desire for security and a reason-able material standard of living truly mirrors the adult, parental culture, but we are perhaps entitled to ask whether this is enough for a nation which may perhaps hope to make a further contribution to civilization, let alone maintain its place as one of the leading countries of the world for scientific and other achievements. Surely it is possible to become too pedestrian. I am still sufficient of a patriot (although I understand the dangers of chauvinism quite clearly) to be stirred by the achievements of a man like Sir Francis Chichester and to feel it an honour to be his fellow countryman.

The dangers of extreme deviance and criminality are much more easily pin-pointed. There are clear signs that juvenile delinquency, youthful drunkenness, drug taking and vandalism are more frequent than they used to be in the more immediate past but whatever their comparative incidence, they present real social problems whose solutions are by no means apparent. There is little point in denying their gravity even though, at the same time, one would want to go on to point out that the vast majority of young people are none of these things and even those of the minority who behave in proscribed ways seldom do so for very long.

The trouble about adolescents is precisely that they are so distinctive and conspicuous a group that they become handy whipping boys for every indignant moralist and over-anxious adult. The more critical comments are made about young people, the more they will be tempted to live up to the warped image. Indeed, one of the disquieting feelings I have about the organization of such a conference as this—in which all the main speakers are over twenty-one to put it mildly!—is that it tends to draw attention to intergenerational differences which are from many points of view better under-emphasized.

At the risk of sounding banal, I would suggest that our principal contribution to youth is first, understanding, and second, respect. The two are inseparable. One of the most helpful ideas I have come across in an attempt at a sociological and psychological understanding of the position of young people today is the concept of the self-image—an idea which is originally derived, I suppose, from Jungian psychology. In the growing-up process we all need to acquire an adequate and valid concept of ourselves—adequate both for our inmost personal needs and for the claims of the social environment. That is what growing up is all about. But not every individual acquires an adequate self-image at the same chronological stage; some, indeed, never seem to do so at all but remain in a confused chrysalis for a large part of their lives. The key orientation of the adolescent is the future. Hence, adolescence is not a self-validating phase at all, and attempts to treat it as such serve merely to prolong irritating absurdities. The three great developmental tasks which young people have to come to terms with and ultimately resolve can be summarized as:

(a) Coming to terms with society, i.e. getting a job, taking part in political and trade-union affairs: in short, fulfilling the role of an adult citizen;

(b) coming to terms with the self, i.e. developing one's talents and capacities, achieving sexual relationships and mature friendships; and

(c) coming to terms with life as a whole, i.e. acquiring a moral code and/or associated religious beliefs and philosophies.

There is always a significant difference between male and female self-images. This is something which classical psychoanalysis overlooked but which a more sophisticated sociological perspective is constantly emphasizing. Boys and girls, of course, have much in common, but when, in adolescence, they look into the future they see themselves playing different social roles and for this reason their attitudes on a number of points are dissimilar. Boys are more concerned about vocations and jobs than girls, while girls seem to focus much more of their attention on getting married and raising a family. The girl says "This is what I hope my life will be like", while the boy more often says "This is what I want to be". The nature of the male role requires boys to achieve a greater degree of independence than is the case for girls. The latter, therefore, do not experience the impulse to rebel against their parents to anything like the same degree. Their self-image is phrased much more than the boys in interpersonal terms.

In this comparison I am, of course, talking in terms of more or less. Youth presents some common developmental problems irrespective of sex. The differential roles, however, produce their own characteristic anxieties and crises. There are, in fact, two adolescent crises, one male and one female, and when it comes to helping young people in the growing-up process whether we are using ordinary educational methods or some more specific form of psycho-social counselling, it is important to remember this truth.

This brings me to what must be my final comments. If there are some specifically adolescent problems arising either from the nature of the developmental phase or as a result of environmental pressures, we will do a disservice to young people if we pretend they do not exist. Is there at this stage a flight into irresponsibility? Is the true adolescent who, in Friedenberg's terms,[10] should face the world with love and defiance, truly vanishing from contemporary society? On the other hand, is the teenage repudiation of conventional values too exaggerated and over-aggressive? Both questions will find some people to answer them affirmatively, and the two questions, both of which pose different issues and spring from conflicting evidence, may be vital ones. They do not necessarily cancel each other out, for some groups of young people may be conformist to the point of passivity, while other groups can be rebellious to a degree that threatens social cohesion. Both the flight into irresponsibility and banality and the reaction of intransigence and flamboyant non-conformity are connived at by certain sections of the community and both receive some institutional support. David Matza[11] has done a service by pointing to the subterranean deviant traditions which link both adult and juvenile communities.

Youth problems then can best be understood in terms of the social roles which young people are obliged to play in our kind of society and also in relation to the differential socialization processes to which they are exposed. The age group becomes the crucial reference group in adolescence partly because it is in the nature of youth that co-operation with peers must take place at that stage. But this is not the whole story. It is also because our society lacks an adequate community-based consensus of moral and social values to sustain a common way of life apart from individualism and egotisms of various sorts. The teenage society and its associated culture are to some extent, then, to be thought of as existing *faute de mieux*.

Fortunately it is not part of my role in this conference to offer prescriptions or to advance policies but I would suggest that, if my analysis is correct, then there are certain general principles which need to be borne in mind. First, that youth needs to be given more not less responsibility, and by this I imply reducing the period of role indeterminacy instead of extending it as we now tend to do. I cannot see any major objections to giving young people the full status of adult citizens at eighteen instead of making them wait until 21.* If we dared to do this some quite drastic rearrangement of our existing educational system would be called for but, since this is in any case long overdue, this would be a general gain. Students in sixth forms and in higher education would be treated as young workers instead of being regarded as over-grown school children as they often are nowadays. Second, and much more important, however difficult to bring about, a greater degree of moral, political and ideological consensus needs to be achieved throughout the community. One cannot but welcome the spirit of ecumenism which seems to be bringing Christians closer together. The next step is for Christians and humanists to establish a viable working relationship. If only we could get our scale and order of values right, then much of the undesirable strain would be removed from our social life. Our public life hardly bears examination and it is no use arraigning youth for qualities and behaviour which are widespread and almost endemic in our society. I must end, therefore, very much as I began, by pleading for our concern for youth not to blind us to the wider problems of living which we all face. Youth does not exist *sui generis* and its alleged problems cannot be understood, much less dealt with, in social isolation. The problems of youth are the problems which face humanity as it seeks to become more civilized; they epitomize in an acute form the pains and stresses of the race as it struggles from its own childhood in search of eventual maturity.

*Written in July 1967 (Eds.)

REFERENCES

1. W. D.WALL, *Child of Our Times*, National Children's Home Convocation Lecture, 1959.
2. R. J. HAVIGHURST *et al.*, *Growing Up In River City*, Wiley, 1962.
3. W. F. WHYTE, *Street Corner Society*, University of Chicago Press, revised edition, 1955.
4. ERIC CLARK, The Great Winter Trek, *The Observer*, 4 October 1964.
5. ALAN SILLITOE, *Saturday Night and Sunday Morning*, Pan, 1960
6. J. B. MAYS, *The Young Pretenders*, Michael Joseph, 1965.
7. PETER LAURIE, *Teenage Revolution*, Blond, 1965.
8. B. JACKSON and D. MARSDEN, *Education and the Working Class*, Routledge and Kegan Paul, 1962 (Pelican edition, 1966).
9. *The Sunday Times*, 13 January 1963.
10. EDGAR FRIEDENBERG *The Vanishing Adolescent*, Dell/Laurel Books, 1962.
11. DAVID MATZA, Subterranean Traditions of Youth, *Annals* of the American Academy of Political and Social Science, November, 1961.

Also for further reading:

COLEMAN, J. *et al.*, *The Adolescent Society*, The Free Press, 1961.

DOUVAN, E. and ADELSON, J., *The Adolescent Experience*, John Wiley, 1966.

EPPEL, E. M. and M., *Adolescents and Morality*, Routledge and Kegan Paul, 1966.

GOETSCHIUS, G. and TASH, J., *Working with Unattached Youth*, Routledge and Kegan Paul, 1967.

HEMMING, J. *Problems of Adolescent Girls*, Heinemann, 1960.

MORSE, MARY, *The Unattached*, Penguin Books, 1965.

MUSGROVE, F., *Youth and the Social Order*, Routledge and Kegan Paul, 1964.

PATEY, E., *Young People Now*, S.C.M., 1964.

ROSENBERG, M., *Society and the Adolescent Self-Image*, Princeton University Press, 1965.

SCHOFIELD, M., *The Sexual Behaviour of Young People*, Longmans, 1965.

SMITH, E. A., *American Youth Culture*, The Free Press, 1962.

WILLMOTT, P., *Adolescent Boys of East London*, Routledge and Kegan Paul, 1966.

CHAPTER 2

The Young Immigrant

FRED MILSON

THE arrival in our midst of large numbers of people of different cultural background and colour in a fairly short period of time is bound to pose problems for the host community as well as for the immigrants themselves. The complexity of the situation should not be obscured by a foolish liberalism which tries to solve problems by pretending they do not exist or by assuming that the problems are entirely of the immigrants' making. It is too easy to argue that if the immigrants were not here there would be no problem; that if they went away, then the problem also would disappear; and that if the immigrants *are* to stay, then "they must not allow themselves to be a problem".

It is also unwise to dismiss as of little significance the sense of cultural shock that both communities feel when confronted one by the other.*

As I turned off the main shopping street, I was immediately overcome with a sense of strangeness, almost of shock . . . what struck one so

---

* The phrase "both communities" over-simplifies the situation, of course. The "community of immigrants" certainly does not form a coherent whole except in so far as the immigrants we are concerned with are all coloured. Exact figures of the numbers of coloured immigrants who have come to Britain are hard to obtain. Probably rather more than three-quarters of a million have arrived since the early fifties to bring the total number of coloured people living in Britain to about 820,000 at the present time. Of these about 430,000 are West Indians; 165,000 are Indians; and 100,000 Pakistanis.

forcefully was that, apart from some shopping housewives and a posse of teddy boys in bright jeans outside the billiard hall, almost everybody in sight had a coloured skin.

It is not only the host community that has been shocked:

> [The immigrants] waited in apathetic misery for someone to tell them what to do. Some leaned over the rail or against the windows, staring with unbelief at the unimaginable prospect outside . . . I overheard . . ."I still can't get over how strange it looks to see the white people working on the railway line, doing the dirty jobs, and cleaning out the toilet: and that white porter, he called me Sir."[1]

Just as the cultural shock confronts both communities, so is each community faced with problems having the same apparent root cause—their involvement in living together—and these problems manifest themselves in different ways for host and immigrant. But whereas we can readily feel how each reacts emotionally to the presence of the other, we find it more difficult to recognize and solve the true nature of the problems which this confrontation presents. This difficulty is more serious for the host community than for the immigrants themselves for the former can so readily (and so understandably) see the immigrants as the whole source of the problems which have arisen.

Clearly there are differences between host and immigrant communities (and, indeed, within each community). Many of these are more than minor irritations at their worst, though they can be stressed disproportionately, but the really major problems, the problems that, if unsolved, can seriously damage our whole society, have been with us for a long time before the first waves of immigrants began to arrive in the early fifties. The coloured immigrant has exposed these flaws in our society—and in us. His presence has a general awareness of already existing problems and, as a result, he has come to bear the full odium for the existence of the problems themselves.

There were "twilight areas" in our cities before the fifties; despite the provisions of the Welfare State there has clearly been a degree of poverty and deprivation that ought not to have been allowed; there has been less opportunity and incentive for some young people than there ought to have been; many of our social services are inadequate in themselves and they are not always effectively organized. And never have our protestations about the absence of colour prejudice in Britain been really put to the test.

Obviously the fairly rapid arrival of three-quarters of a million coloured immigrants has intensified these problems, but instead of wishing the problems would go away we would be better employed in trying to solve them at their root—in our own society and in ourselves. Once we have settled our minds to the fact that the major problems are going to be with us whether the immigrants are in Bradford or Bombay, Birmingham or Barbados, we might even find time to be thankful that the immigrants have brought forward the *opportunity* of doing something about these problems before they have been allowed to fester through neglect.

We shall not, even with the best will in the world, solve every problem overnight; social attitudes and personal feelings cannot be changed by Act of Parliament. We can, however, make a start on tackling these problems and our greatest hope of success lies where we shall find our greatest challenge—with the young immigrant.

THE YOUNG IMMIGRANT

There are many reasons why young immigrants are most vulnerable to these pressures. Those who have arrived in this country with most or all of their schooling completed have to find their way in this society when their most formative years and their social education have been spent in another culture. An extreme example is a sub-group of Indian adolescent boys known to the writer. They came to this country with their parents when they were 13, 14 and 15—nobody is clear of their exact age. There is very little if any formal schooling for them in this country, they speak different Indian dialects and have to learn English to communicate even with each other. They are on the threshold of adulthood in a society for which they have had no training.

Yet severe as these problems may be, the present generation of teenagers is still protected by the customs they and their parents have brought with them.[2] In several important respects the "second generation teenage immigrants" (those born here or who were brought here in early childhood and have most of their schooling in this country) are more vulnerable still. If they go through the English educational and socialization process, they will identify themselves as "Young Englanders". They will have higher expectations than their predecessors and rejection or discrimination on the grounds of colour will be felt more keenly. Moreover the two-culture clash is more serious for them. Problems become acute when home and society represent different worlds each with its own pattern of accepted behaviour.

For both groups of young immigrants there is already undeniable evidence of colour discrimination in employment.[3] The writer was assured in one city that it was impossible to employ coloured girls on food counters since this would be unacceptable to the customers. When he asked whether this belief had ever been tested, as coloured girls were serving food in other cities, there was no reply.

Of course, one of the problems of identifying colour prejudice directed against young immigrants is that many of the problems they face are created by social factors. They live in areas where most youngsters leave school at 15, go into semi-skilled and unskilled jobs, do not join youth organizations and suffer the deprivations of overcrowded conditions.[4]

A problem, however, does not disappear when we cannot define its exact boundaries. There is plenty of evidence to show that there is racial discrimination in Britain and that many coloured youngsters experience unusual difficulty in adjusting to society and finding their true place in life. Common sense suggests that there is an urgency in the question and that time is not on our side. Not only do second generation immigrants have higher expectations but numbers will grow. At present the coloured teenagers are a relatively small proportion of the whole, but this will increase. Birmingham, for example, has hundreds of coloured teenagers in 1967: by 1977 it will have thousands.* If discontent is rife among this group they could

* The situation will be much worse in some areas than even these numbers suggest. As is well known, in large conurbations a particular neighbourhood—

constitute a major social problem. Furthermore, if coloured people are allowed to slip into a position of social inferiority then that position will become self-perpetuating.

What can the Youth Service do?

THE HUNT COMMITTEE—AIMS

In December 1965 a subcommittee of the Youth Service Development Council was set up under the chairmanship of Lord (then Sir John) Hunt to "consider the part which the Youth Service might play in meeting the needs of young immigrants in England and Wales and to make recommendations". Early in its work the committee found it necessary to define its social goals.

The committee rejected the idea of segregated communities; it rejected the concept of "accommodation between the communities"; and it rejected total assimilation of the immigrants. What was envisaged was that *both* sides should change and adapt. The report, *Immigrants and the Youth Service*, actually states:

> Para. 43: We reject the idea of several *segregated* societies, because this implies that the immigrants should be kept and maintained as separate entities, with social intercourse between them and the host community restricted both by law and by custom. This pattern is unacceptable to us on moral grounds. A second alternative is the concept of *accommodation* between the immigrant and host communities. This has been defined by Rashmi Desai* as a situation in which "immigrants accept the relationships available to them and act on them with some degree of conformity, but do not share the bulk of attitudes which are part of the host society." This idea, too, we reject, for we do not believe it to be a satisfactory relationship between people. A third choice is the *assimilation of* immigrants to the host society. This is a situation in which, as Mr. Desai describes it, "immigrants come to share . . . the attitudes, behaviour and values of the social group within the host society with which they identify themselves."

---

usually of poorer, older dwelling houses—has a much higher proportion of immigrants than other neighbourhoods. Thus, Birmingham with a total population of 1,100,000 now has 70,000 coloured immigrants. In some areas they make up at least 50 per cent of the population although in the middle-class suburbs on the outskirts of the city a coloured family is scarcely to be found.

* R. S. Desai, *Indian Immigrants in Britain*. O.U.P., 1963.

This concept, also, we reject. It requires immigrants to give up their own background and become entirely absorbed in the culture and values of the host society. Such a solution could only be imposed at very great personal and social cost. Further, it presents a one-sided picture of the situation, with immigrants adapting to the host society, while the host society remains unchanged. We envisage, rather, that in the course of learning to live together, both sides will change and adapt.[5]

The committee accepted as its long-term aim the definition of integration given by the Home Secretary, on 23 May 1966:

I do not regard integration as meaning the loss, by immigrants, of their own national characteristics and culture. I do not think that we need in this country a "melting pot", which will turn everybody out in a common mould, as one of a series of carbon copies of someone's misplaced vision of the stereotyped Englishman . . . .I define integration, therefore, not as a flattening process of assimilation but as equal opportunity, accompanied by cultural diversity, in an atmosphere of mutual tolerance. This is the goal. We may fall a little short of its full attainment, as have other communities both in the past and the present. But if we are to maintain any sort of world reputation for civilized living and social cohesion, we must get far nearer to its achievement than is the case to-day.[6]

The committee went a little further in defining what it understood by integration:

Young immigrants, whatever their origins and whether or not the United Kingdom is to be their permanent home, should be able to settle happily in this country without prejudice and in close relationship with the indigenous population, and that they should be able to enjoy the social and recreational amenities they prefer, find work according to their individual capacities and so contribute to the life of the whole community. This is what we understand by integration.[7]

The acceptance of this goal would challenge the complacency encountered in some parts of the country. In one area the writer was assured, "All is well. We have no problems. We treat coloured youngsters like the rest." That same evening, coloured teenagers told a different story. They were meeting discrimination in education, employment, leisure and friendship groups.

People are fond of quoting the "Burns-night analogy"; Scots away from home associate with other Scots. But this is to fail to recognize how different are the two social situations. The Scots away from home have at least equal opportunities with the natives. Their association is a first free choice. The coloured immigrant may be compelled to seek ethnic groups, because full acceptance is withheld elsewhere.[8]

PROSPECTS

Can the Youth Service be an agent in the process of integration as it has been defined above? The Hunt Report is optimistic.

> We are convinced that the Youth Service has a special role to play . . . . It can bring young people together in their leisure time and through shared activities, provide opportunities for friendship and mutual understanding, which will be valuable to them in the mixed community in which they find themselves.[9]

But faced with the evidence, the members of the committee admitted the reality was most discouraging.

> . . . over and above any shortage of Youth Service facilities, we detect a lack of awareness of the special needs of young immigrants, almost a "take it or leave it" attitude, which is no better for being based on the philosophy that to make any special effort is itself a form of discrimination.[10]

True, there are particular groups and even communities which have an impressive record of integration. On the whole it seems uniformed organizations are more likely to be successful with the coloured immigrants, especially the younger teenagers. These organizations offer a clear programme of activities and do not, as often in the club, leave the youngster to find acceptance in a social and recreational setting. They were often at work in the country from which the immigrant has come. The common uniform has a levelling effect. There is evidence too that courses in further education have an appeal particularly if they offer the rewards of recognition for skill and knowledge. But the overall picture is depressing. Once again it is hard to say how much of this is due to colour and how much is owed to the fact that these coloured youngsters belong to a social class which is underprivileged. *Youth Service is not conspicuously successful in its appeal to white youngsters in similar social circumstances.*[11]

RECOMMENDATIONS

(a) Social attitudes

The report was emphatic about the need for a change in social attitudes:

> If there is one single recommendation, applying at all levels, which emerged from our report it is this: there is a need for a new attitude in our society towards immigrants, a conscious desire to create a new society.[12]

The report could hardly be specific about the social changes it thought desirable. Nevertheless the concern for a change in attitudes and its recommendations regarding the Youth Service are important since they point to the limitations on the power of the Youth Service as an agent of integration. To put the matter extremely, it would be impossible to have "an integrated Youth Service and a segregated society." Any integrating process within Youth Service will require considerable supports from the community outside.

(b) Improvements in the operation of Youth Service

The report then calls for a new initiative for integration within the Youth Service itself among members, voluntary and statutory bodies, local and national powers. There is a declaration of intent that separate ethnic groups are not to be encouraged. A dynamic situation demands that we have integrated youth groups from the beginning, however painful this situation may be now. There are references to training, sports equipment and the need for a field officer to encourage integration among the young in areas where immigrants are a high proportion of the total population. There can be little doubt that in certain areas, the acceptance of this challenge would of itself transform Youth Service and give it point and purpose.

(c) **Links with social agencies**

Finally, the needs of young immigrants are seen in an interprofessional setting:

> We have stressed throughout this report . . . that meeting the needs of young immigrants should not be viewed in the limited context of the Youth Service. We have to consider the life of the immigrant as a whole.[13]

Thus the youth worker must be a partner with teachers, librarians, youth employment officers, lecturers in colleges of further education, social workers, and—not least—with immigrants themselves and their parents. There are so many variations in the immigrants' situation—from city to city, and between one part of the city and another—that in many cases the way forward can only be found by the mobilization of neighbourhood resources—and conscience. The conscientious youth worker must resist the temptation "to go it alone". It would be a pity if the young immigrants exchanged the segregation of colour for the segregation of an age group.

There is a growing consensus of opinion in this country in favour of interprofessional study, training and work among social and educational workers. It is a fact that there is overlapping and wastage through the present fragmentation and isolation. The question has also been raised whether the traditional roles of social workers are not changing under present conditions. The acceptance of the multi-racial challenge in our society, represented by the growing population of young coloured citizens, would of itself encourage interprofessionalism.

REFERENCES

1. Both quotations are from SHEILA PATTERSON, *Dark Strangers*, Pelican 1965, pp. 13–15.
2. *Young and Coloured*. A Survey by the Youth Development Trust, Manchester, 1967.
3. *Ibid.*
4. See *Operation Integration II*, Westhill Occasional Paper, 1966. But the Sparkbrook Survey, *Race, Community and Conflict—A Study of Sparkbrook*,

(O.U.P., 1967), by JOHN REX and ROBERT MOORE found the handicap of race and colour to be the main difficulty.

5. D.E.S., *Immigrants and the Youth Service*, H.M.S.O., 1967,
6. *Ibid.* para. 44.
7. *Ibid.* para. 45.
8. cf. *Operation Integration I*, Westhill Occasional Paper, 1965.
9. *Ibid.* para. 130.
10. *Ibid.* para. 138.
11. G. GOETSCHIUS and J. TASH, *Working with Unattached Youth*, Routledge and Kegan Paul, 1967; see also MARY MORSE, *The Unattached*, Pelican, 1965.
12. *Ibid.* para. 268.
13. *Ibid.* para. 247.

CHAPTER 3

The Development of Youth Service within the Context of the Social Services

D. C. MARSH

THE fact that one of the main topics for discussion at this conference is the relationship of the Youth Service to other particular kinds of services, such as the probation and the education services, implies that the Youth Service is somehow separate from the social services as a whole. This separation of particular kinds of services from each other is of course by no means unusual in our Welfare State. Indeed, one of the strongest criticisms which can be made of the growth and development of our social services is that all too frequently a new service is developed without any real thought having been given to its relationship with the other services already in being or projected. And this, of course, is why in recent years we have heard so much about the need for co-ordination; and why we had a Minister of the Crown charged with the sole function of making plans for co-ordination apparently without success, which does not surprise me, because any attempt to co-ordinate must inevitably under our system of organization and administration come up against an enormous variety of obstacles, most of which cannot easily be removed, even by the government.* What, then, is the point of worrying about co-ordination? Would it be wiser, and indeed would it not be more profitable, for us to ask fundamental questions such as, are all the social services, as we know them now, really necessary? If so, how should they be financed, organized and administered? How can they be provided with sufficient flexibility so as to meet the ever changing aspirations and needs of society?

* Written in 1967 (Eds.)

Those kinds of questions would lead us immediately to a consideration of the role and function of the Youth Service in this country, and let me therefore begin by asking, provocatively, "Is a Youth Service really necessary?" Most of you would doubtless say "Yes, without question", but a case could be made out that there is no real need, and certainly not much demand, for a Youth Service. Indeed, it could be argued that a number of other services such as education, social security, child care, probation, and youth employment are all concerned with the needs of youth, so why then try and develop a Youth Service?

Of one fact we can be certain and that is that our society in modern times has been ambivalent about the need for a Youth Service. Successive governments in the last thirty odd years have paid lip service to the need for and the assumed value of such a service, but as was clearly shown in the report of the Albemarle Committee[1] very little was done either by the central government or most local authorities to develop the service between 1944 and 1958. Was this simply due to lack of funds, as the committee tactfully suggested, or was it in fact due to a lack of faith in the value of a Youth Service?

Lady Albemarle and her colleagues were absolutely convinced that a real Youth Service can be of great value and "is deeply relevant to the needs and complexities of a modern society". But I have still to be convinced of the validity of many of the arguments used in their report. However, that is not to say that there is no case for firmly establishing a Youth Service; what bothers me is that there are a number of basic problems which need to be resolved before we can justify and design a proper service.

For example, are we as yet clear as to what we mean by the term "youth"? We now use a variety of chronological ages for many different purposes to delimit the freedom of young people, with the result that in some age ranges they are regarded as "youths" for some purposes and not for others. We must recognize, far more clearly than we have done, that lengthening the span of compulsory education, the influence of mass media, and so on make the young person of today very different from the person of his or her age even 30 years ago. Yet we still use the same kinds of age limits today as we did in the past. Perhaps the Latey Report[2] will shed some light on this problem when it is published, but until we resolve issues of these kinds how can we fully justify and design a service for undefined youth?

The other basic problem seems to me to be that of identifying the needs of youth. For too long we have gone on relying on the hunches of older generations as to what the needs of youth are when it is abundantly clear that what was necessary in my youth would certainly not satisfy the needs of modern youth. We acquire far more systematic research into the genuine needs of young people, especially normal young people and not just the drug takers and the beatniks. Research in this field would need to be continuous because social conditions and the aspirations of young people are changing more rapidly now than ever before. One could go on discussing problems of these kinds, but let us assume that we have decided that a Youth Service is desirable and so go on to consider the real topic I was asked to talk about, and that is how to fit a Youth Service more effectively into the pattern of the social services as a whole.

In recent years, the social services have yet again become a subject of controversy, but I regret to say that there seems to be very little fundamental thinking about the role and methods of organization of the social services. Some of us have argued for years that unless we have a comprehensive and exhaustive examination of the social services as a whole and not just of some of the parts from time to time, then we will never devise systematic social policies and measures for their implementation. Many of you will know better than I do of existing defects, but let me highlight what seem to me to be some of the salient features of our system of social services.

The first is our lack of clarity of definitions and aims. That is to say that even today there is no real unanimity as to what are or are not social services. There is no need for me to elaborate on this point, I have done so at length elsewhere. What does bother me is that because of the absence of any systematic definition of the aims and purposes of social policy and of the social services, we are now beginning to be led back into the situation where we are being asked to accept that the social services should in effect be publicly provided only for the poor. The suggestions being made, for example, by some groups of economists, that all who can pay individually for, say, health and education services, and retirement pensions should do so, clearly imply that publicly provided services should only be made available for the poor. Again, I do not want to enter into a lengthy debate on these suggestions, having done so elsewhere, but I do want to discuss briefly the principles implied in proposals of these kinds. In effect, these proposals mean the abolition of the social services as most of us would understand that term. And as far as youth services are concerned they, too, would presumably have to be bought individually and provided "free" only for those who cannot afford to pay. In short, back to the old days of charitable clubs for the slum-dweller.

There is obviously a minority of the population which would be prepared to pay individually so as to have a greater "choice in Welfare", but the majority want services socially provided. The real problem is that as a society we still have no coherent social policy, and until we do have one the present controversy over universality and selectivity seems to me to be rather irrelevant.

The original development of our social services (undefined, of course) was based on selectivity. For example, the first non-contributory old-age pension scheme was highly selective; so too was the first scheme of national insurance against sickness and unemployment; and when secondary education was first publicly provided it was limited to a very small proportion of the school-age population. It was not until we began to plan for post-war reconstruction in the 1940's, and then proceeded to establish the Welfare State (as most people seem to believe) in the years 1944–48, that we accepted the principle of universality. Now, however, we seem to be having second thoughts about the practicability of applying that principle, especially in relation to those services designed to deal with the problems of financial poverty. What worries me is that all too often discussions of principles are concerned wholly with finance and not with social justice and social responsibilities.

Clearly, any decisions made about basic principles are bound to affect the Youth Service. If selectivity is to be applied will there be a Youth Service at all within the context of the statutory social services? Presumably not, and the only hope would be through voluntary organizations or commercial enterprises.

The last salient feature of our social services which we must consider concerns the methods of organization and administration. If we had deliberately planned to make the organizations so complex as to be unintelligible to ordinary mortals we could not possibly have been as successful as we have been without any overall planning. Just think of the varieties of organizational patterns which now exist for the making and implementing of social policies. We use central government departments, local government departments, and *ad hoc* boards in weird and wonderful ways. I find it difficult to see how any foreign visitor who comes to this country to examine our social services ever manages to work his way through the maze of what I once described as "a hotchpotch of administrative units, a tangle of legislative complexity and a jungle of vested interests". It is not just the complexity which I find disturbing, it is the inequalities which follow. The fact, for example, that standards of provision for primary and secondary education may vary from excellent to downright bad; and that national policies may hardly be implemented at all in some areas. The latter was clearly revealed in the Albemarle Report where it was shown that even in 1958 "some important authorities have no youth committee and no youth service officer". The report revealed a fantastic variation in expenditure on Youth Services.

Variety we are told has value, but surely not when it leads to situations of the extreme kinds we can find in the organization and financing of the social services. No one in their right minds would want absolute uniformity throughout the country so that, for example, every member of every youth club in every part of the country attended precisely the same kind of club and did precisely the same activity every Monday at 6.30 p.m. But, equally one cannot approve of the gross discrepancies in provision where, for example, one area may have excellent facilities for youth and a neighbouring area may have none at all.

How these complexities and discrepancies can be removed depends on a variety of factors and forces. Above all, they depend on the sincerity of politicians and administrators in ensuring that national policies are effectively implemented; on a drastic reform of local government, and on the eradication of myths concerning local democracy and the assumed altruistic intentions of pressure groups and vested interests.

Even if the desired reforms were brought about, there still remains the vexed question of "functional" boundaries between services. At present, the child-care services are deemed to be quite distinct from those of youth employment, or probation and even education, and these examples can be multiplied over and over again. But should each be quite separate from the other? The reason for the separateness of each of the services is that they have been developed piece-meal and have tended to become compartmentalized even when they may be dealing with the same problem. Equally, we have tended to develop separatist social workers, so that probation officers are assumed to be quite different from child-care officers, mental welfare officers different from psychiatric and medical social workers, and so on, *ad infinitum*. Are the differences real, and is the degree of expertise in one so very much greater than that in another? I doubt it, and surely of all people social workers should be above compartmentalism and petty jealousies of status. Where, one wonders, does the unfortunate youth officer fit into the hierarchical structure of social work; indeed, is he a social worker?

At long last we are beginning to recognize that so many of these divisions are artificial and unnecessary, but what solutions are we being offered for the problems of assumed distinctive functions? One is to establish a social service for the family on the lines of the Kilbrandon Report for Scotland and the vague white paper (now buried we hope) in England. If, however, a family social service is impracticable, where do we go from there?

I would like to see the social services organized on a regional basis under central government control. Fears of bureaucracy and inflexibility are, in my view, greatly exaggerated; indeed I have seen far more petty bureaucratic tyranny in some small town halls than I have ever seen in Whitehall. In the regions, and then in districts, I would like to see a comprehensive social welfare department, obviously with its specialist divisions but not rigidly divided by insurmountable and supposedly functional boundaries. What services should be included is an open question, though there are obvious cases for integration. The final solution, however, depends on our determining the real aims and function of social policy and its implementation through the social services, but no doubt you would want to see the Youth Service incorporated. Or would you?

I am not sure, as I said to begin with, whether a Youth Service as such is now necessary. In view of the fact that we are prolonging the length of education, that all sorts of other services have a bearing on youth, and that the mass media are largely youth oriented, I am left wondering what is, or should be, the role of a Youth Service. Clearly, we still need far more recreational facilities and opportunities for young people than we have at present, and we need to find, perhaps above all else, a means of bridging the gap between school and the real world. Could a Youth Service offer these services, and if so how and in what way would such services be provided and organized? I end, therefore, with questions which I hope you will answer.

REFERENCES

1. MINISTRY OF EDUCATION, *The Youth Service in England and Wales* ('Albemarle Report'), H.M.S.O., 1960.
2. COMMITTEE ON THE AGE OF MAJORITY *Report* ('Latey Report'), Cmnd. 3342, H.M.S.O., 1967.

PART TWO

YOUTH SERVICE AND RELATED EDUCATIONAL AND SOCIAL PROVISION

The following papers explore the relationships between Youth Service and four neighbouring professional areas— the schools, further education, probation, and youth employment. Their separate historical development but complementary and often overlapping functions are discussed; and the possible operational advantages and economies of interprofessional training for the related but distinctive roles of youth leader, teacher, probation officer and youth employment officer, are also considered.

CHAPTER 4

The Relationship of Schools and Youth Service

A. N. FAIRBAIRN

I BELIEVE that it goes without saying that there is, and must continue to be a relationship between schools and Youth Service if for no other reason than that they exist to meet the needs of the same age groups of young people and that they often operate in each other's premises. I propose, therefore, to discuss in this paper, first, the needs of young people which both are trying to serve; second, the relationship as it exists now; and third, how it might be more effectively developed.

I shall devote most of my time to this latter area, first because a Committee of the Youth Service Development Council is currently studying this subject;* and second, because I believe that the service ought to be essentially an "action" set-up and that youth workers want to assess for themselves and in relation to the possibilities and limitations of their own local organization or club, practical suggestions which they can either implement, amend or discard.

Of course, youth workers must keep in the forefront of their minds and be continually developing their professional aims in the service of the needs and aspirations of young people; but in order to carry these out effectively, I submit that they must know far more intimately and keep abreast of as assiduously as their time will permit, the work of the secondary schools. In particular, they need to know something of the way in which the curriculum is developing, and of the attitudes of teachers and the nature of experiments in close co-operation between schools and Youth Service up and down

* Written in 1967 (Eds.)

the country, in order to be able to influence the schools and to understand some of the background of the young school leaver who comes to them after school or work.

The schools and Youth Service exist to serve the needs of young people in different but complementary ways, and both must aim to do this within a community setting. Indeed, it may with justification be said that both schools and youth organizations are different, but linked branches of service to the community. Put another way, I suppose it would be generally agreed that both would be the poorer and more misguided if they paid no attention to the nature of the community in which they found themselves. So in general terms they exist to serve the needs of young people within a mainly local community context. Perhaps this is all the more important, as was said in a recent issue of the journal *Trends in Education* on the subject of the community school:

> The way in which we are rebuilding Britain, the creation of more and more massive new communities on the edges of our cities is changing the pattern of life of great numbers of people. Many of these estates tend to be cut off, both physically and socially from the city of which they are a part. They are cultural deserts within which, only very slowly, is the germ of community feeling beginning to grow. One pressing need is for the development of a focus of some kind, to encourage this growth. One way in which this is being done in some areas is to develop schools much more for the whole community.

The motive behind these efforts has perhaps been summed up best by Professor Phillips as follows:

> When the school's role was relatively monolithic in character—teaching children to read, write and compute—little attention was paid to it as an institution influencing values. Today its role has become pluralistic. In one respect its task is clear. It must take reponsibility for bringing the child into communication with problems which demand solution through the use of the new social sciences, sciences and arts, and this new dimension demands a new intellectual unity and coherence. But at the same time, new demands are being made on the school at the points of home–school relations, after-school activities, work and leisure, emotional and social counselling. Here there is need for reappraisal so that a haphazard accretion of tasks can be replaced by a planned, conscious assessment of the school's new role.[1]

What then are the needs of young people which schools and Youth Service exist to serve? I do not think there is any one hard and fast answer to this. So much depends on the needs of individuals, on the state of society at any moment of time, and so on. This is reflected in the differences in presentation between, for instance, Sir John Maud's definition in 1949 and that set out in the Crowther Report of 1959. The first reads as follows:

> To offer to individual young people, in their leisure time, opportunities of various kinds, complementary to those of home, formal education and work, to discover and develop their personal resources of body, mind and spirit and thus better equip themselves to live the life of mature, creative and responsible members of society.

The second (from Crowther) is really describing the four areas which ought to be the concern of county colleges, and these were:

(1) to develop an appreciation and understanding of the adult world;

(2) to provide guidance in working out human relationships and moral standards;

(3) to assist in the development of physical and aesthetic skills;

(4) to continue basic education with a vocational bias where appropriate.[2]

Again, we would be false to ourselves if we saw these needs as being fulfilled solely by the secondary schools and Youth Service. They must surely be seen within the wider context of community, parents, social services and so on. Young people need to grasp what the world is all about, and how they can adequately meet its demands at various stages of their existence. They want to learn how to live in society, effect change, select and make choice, and effect personal relationships reasonably easily. All that I have said so far about needs might be described as what adults consider to be the needs of young people. There are also two other ways of looking at these needs—namely, how young people themselves assess their needs, and also those factors which might be described as *basic* needs.

To take the last named first, I suppose the need for identity, security, acceptance, appreciation and creativity, all dependent on experience, are as comprehensive a list as one requires. But what of the views of the young people themselves? Surveys, like that very interesting Shantasea example carried out by Fred Milson and Westhill College of Education, do not show a massively articulate youth or an impressive shopping list of unrequited needs. I do not think this is any reason for the adult to be cynical, but rather to look more closely at the two needs in which young people universally express interest; first, experience based on meeting or getting to know other people, and second, earning the wherewithal to get into contact with other people.

These, then, are but a few thoughts on the basic question of the needs of young people. I simply want to suggest that just occasionally youth workers, teachers, parents and indeed anyone whose life or work brings them into constant contact with young people, ought to sit down quietly and reflect on the subject of needs as relating to their particular group of youngsters.

What is the relationship at present existing between Youth Service and schools? It is exceptionally difficult to be exact on this, because there is simply no comprehensive statistical data available, nor have there been any serious studies on the subject. The former would have been extremely difficult to assess, and the latter reflects in some measure anyway the three major isolating factors in the history and development of Youth Service itself. Firstly in the nineteenth century, the development of the voluntary organizations mirrored their concern for the depressed social conditions of the young working poor. This was even more marked after the passage of the 1870 Education Act which planted fairly and squarely on the school boards and the Board of Education, responsibility for universal elementary education. It was their job to deal with literacy and numeracy which were therefore in a sense separated from the business of raising the social dignity of young people. Secondly, the initiation of the Youth Service as such by Circular 1486 in 1939, under the stimulus of imminent war, in retrospect looks like an isolated action forced by a perfectly understandable piece of national expediency. Thus, Circular 1486 tended to underline the continuing apartness of the Youth Service from the other branches of the Education Service.[3] Thirdly, the Albemarle Report, in some measure emphasized the separateness of the service. Like the previous isolating factors in the history of the Youth Service which I have quoted, this was not done deliberately or consciously. Indeed the report aimed to eradicate a previous period of gross neglect by the Ministry of Education, brought to light by the investigations of the Select Committee on Estimates of the House of Commons in 1957. But in making the government produce annual £3–£4 million Youth Service building programmes, set up a college for the training of youth leaders, and implement a number of important reforms, the report tended to stress once again the separateness of Youth Service.[4]

The developments of the last 100 years have therefore, been largely geared to effecting a service for young people who have left school. Only very recently, indeed under the sledge-hammer blows of such major pieces of biological and educational fact like the population explosion of the last ten years ($1\frac{1}{2}$ million more children in school by 1980 than at the present time), the achievement of secondary education for all and the planned raising of the school leaving age in 1970, have we been forced to seriously reconsider the position and task of the Youth Service as we at present see it. On the analogy that a team of horses draws most efficiently when trotting at the pace of its slowest member, basic considerations reorienting Youth Service towards a service for the young people in local communities involving a much more serious consideration of what goes on before in secondary schools and afterwards in further education, will only really get underway when those engaged in Youth Service, and public opinion itself, see the practical reality and common sense of so doing. Of course, there are quite a number of areas where conscious and successful attempts have been made to structure schools and further education as a natural and attractive progression for young people. These areas are likely to be the pace-makers in the next chapter of educational and social development for the 14–30 age group, which will undoubtedly have to concentrate on the provision of an effective and integrated local leisure service.

There is much which could be said about the lack of human contacts between schools and Youth Service at the present time (with the exception of course of those pacemakers to which I referred earlier). The great majority of the occupants of secondary school staffrooms, let alone of primary schools, are quite ignorant about youth work other than as a name, or of the actual provision in their localities, probably not thinking of scouts and guides as part of Youth Service at all, despite their own membership of them at an early age. They express resentment at the use of their practical rooms by youth clubs, and in many cases even when involved in a voluntary or part-time capacity are not particularly clear about its aims and objects. In Youth Service itself, there will be a signal ignorance of the rapidly developing and changing curriculum in secondary schools, especially under the impending influence of 1970; possibly an unclear appreciation of further education, vocational and non-vocational opportunities in the neighbourhood; an unwillingness to persevere with recalcitrant heads of evening institutes, who on the first occasion were not helpful in suggesting names of teachers or in providing the practical facilities for special activities for youth groups; and still, in certain cases, a feeling of blind resentment of school teachers because they are held responsible "for letting us have the leftovers". This latter sentiment is still quite prevalent and it has been voiced to me just as often by full-time youth leaders, as by part-time ones.

I want now to explore some of the ways in which there can be a closer and more fruitful relationship between schools and Youth Service. I might add that I am not advocating this closer relationship simply for its own sake, or because it may be the "fashionable" thing to do, but because I honestly believe that the lives of the whole range of young people between 14 and 20 or thereabouts can be immensely enriched if there is a little more liaison between the partners, and a more effective use made of existing and proposed capital resources for schools and adult education and Youth Service. In a sense Youth Service since 1961 has been limited by what it could squeeze from the Youth Service building programme, and, building programmes of any kind never provide enough money to do what you want to do.

Youth Service has recently done a good deal of jumping on

bandwagons, whose directions and objects its passengers do not always understand or appreciate. This is very often due to the lack of communication of objectives down into and across the service, and it is most important that there should not be a breakdown in communication of objectives of this sort in any description of the need to improve relationships between Youth Service and schools. Everything which now follows presupposes a willingness by Youth Service workers to come to grips with the nature of the task of education in the secondary schools; and an equal willingness by teachers to appreciate the general aims and objectives of youth organisations in their localities. To do this, both sides must know each other personally, and must find time to consult each other in a fully professional manner over their common problems, aspirations and aims.

I would venture one generalization here, namely that youth workers ought to understand as far as they can the backcloth of comprehensive secondary education which is spreading over the country and which will offer wide opportunities of educational development to far greater numbers of children than is possible under the tripartite system. The numerous examples of children passing through a comprehensive system and on to higher educational opportunities of one sort or another, who had been adjudged at 11+ to have I.Q.s of 110 or below, are now legion, and the substantial increase of the 15+ age group staying on at the comprehensive school voluntarily, is quite remarkable. Both these examples illustrate a number of encouraging factors within what will become an increasingly flexible secondary education system, and one which stimulates the academic and aptitudinal mobility of children within the secondary schools. I therefore predict that the number of cases of complaint from youth workers that the schools send them the "rejects" ought to decrease.

Yet apart from the improvement of secondary organization, I believe that in secondary education we are now engaged in a great period of curriculum reappraisal and discussion. The education of the whole child for work and leisure is the objective pursued by an increasing number of teachers. There is also a growing awareness of the school's obligations to its local community which demands, *par excellence*, a more broadly spread knowledge of the geography of local industries and of local further education and recreational opportunities. Let me illustrate this by an example in the field of work and careers. In Leicestershire since 1963, we have done all in our power to bring together education and industry, as a direct result of that long since forgotten venture N.P.Y. A number of practical schemes have been mapped out by a working party consisting of executives, trade unionists, the youth employment service and teachers, to make liaison more continuously effective. One of these schemes was the initiation of a programme for the secondment of secondary teachers to local industries for one week at a time. This was born of the conviction that the form master or mistress ought to have a good first-hand working knowledge of modern industrial processes, in order to be able to answer the odd but nevertheless vital *ad hoc* question by pupils. In the increasingly large secondary schools of today, the chances of a youngster getting a substantial period of careers guidance with the careers teacher or Y.E.O. are somewhat limited. Again, a cementing of the bonds of contact between teachers and children would follow if it was apparent to the pupil that the teacher really knew something about the shop floor and the hurly burly of industrial life from which the parents of the majority of his charges come, and from whence most of the latter would go when they left school—a state of affairs very uncommon amongst teachers purely through lack of opportunity. Last winter, 140 teachers were seconded and the same number will go next winter. We ought to be able to give all our secondary teachers a similar period of secondment within five years. There are a number of organizational and background experiments of this type beginning to get underway in the country at large.

But in addition, the proposed raising of the school-leaving age has resulted in a ferment of thought in secondary schools about how best to reshape the curriculum to take account of the extra year. The Schools Council and the Nuffield Foundation publications are the national pointers in this revolutionary approach. They harness a number of new technological developments in the way of "educational hardware" and seek to develop new approaches to the curriculum by team teaching methods and the like. But they all have in common the determination to forge a more vital and relevant 5-year course for all abilities, and in respect of the ability range below the 75th percentile, i.e. the non-academics, all are determined to do everything they can to relate the last years of the curriculum to the realities of the world of work and leisure into which the school leaver will go.

At this point, may I exemplify some of the new approaches to the curriculum being developed in the secondary schools, and also some aspects of the subjects and activities themselves so as to point out their absolutely vital follow-through potential for youth workers. I believe it is crucial for youth workers to know not only that a school plays soccer and net-ball, excels in certain aspects of music, drama and art, but just why it so excels, and the curriculum approach its teams of teachers have adopted in order to ensure that the after school opportunities in Youth Service and further education may be developed in a way conducive to the young person's continued active participation and enjoyment of these skills. Just to offer an activity on the grounds that youth club members did it at school, and without any more critical background knowledge of how the school tackled it, is almost certainly inviting failure. Again, in many cases it is fairly obvious after the shortest survey of the local facilities that a failure to continue certain favourite activities after leaving school is closely linked to the fact that only the local school or schools possess the facilities for continuation.

The approach to physical activities in schools has changed considerably since the war, and most particularly in the development of a widening range of minority sports in addition to the more traditional team games. There has always been a substantial reduction of young people's participation in physical activities after leaving school and there is no reason to believe that the falling off is any greater now than twenty years ago. However, those responsible for the development of these activities are, I believe, motivated by far wider and catholic attitudes than before the war. On the other hand, there are a number of factors which do not make the development of physical activities in the secondary schools straightforward. Not least of these are the problems of the lack of field and indoor game spaces in many schools, and also the exceedingly rapid turnover of female P.E. staff due to early marriage which radically affects the popularity of girls' sports. Such problems predicate a more liberal attitude to the development of physical activities in secondary schools. The construction of large semi-open and semi-heated sports hall areas and swimming baths, especially where large schools are being built or created by extension gives the opportunity to develop the minority sports like archery, badminton, fencing, trampolining, basketball, golf, volleyball, table-tennis, national dancing and so on. Increasing numbers of authorities are acquiring outdoor pursuits centres in the National Parks of this country, where such activities as climbing, trekking, hiking, sailing, canoeing, etc., can be developed for small groups. But in the case of minority sports, a school's resources will never be able to cope fully with all demands and thus I would advocate the development of the closest contact possible with local voluntary sports clubs, and commercial facilities. Schools and youth organizations could well exploit such local independent commercial resources as horse riding, golf, ski training, and ice skating. Such local resources have a potential of skilled coaches who might well be willing to be involved in the secondary school situation, whilst at the same time preparing the way for continued contact after school with sport.

All these thoughts on physical activities indicate that they are essentially bridging activities between school and the adult world. It is important that the work of the regional and local sports councils take all these factors into account as well as Youth Service itself. My message to youth organizations in this sphere, in as far as I ought to be rash and generalize, is that individual organizations ought to try to offer one or two popular sports as a standard part of their programme, e.g. soccer and table-tennis, and for the rest, aim to ascertain the interests of individual members. If these cannot be met within existing local resources, then they can be put in touch with local organizations who can provide for an individual's needs.

Let me now turn to another curriculum subject example, music.

One would think that in great associative activities like instrumental music-making and in the choral sphere in particular they ought to commence with a head start because at least half the population can sing if a stimulating and interesting approach has been made to the subject at school. What are the problems? First, the training of teachers, where, except at two or three specialist colleges of education, music has been largely confined to the needs of the primary school. There are comparatively few music rooms in secondary schools; practically no attention is paid to the provision of musical instruments, record players or records in schools; and music is generally dropped in the last years of secondary school life because of the excuse of examination pressures. It is significant that if music is dropped in the middle years of the secondary school, it is extremely difficult for the individual to pick it up again in later life. Science, woodwork and metal work, domestic science, art and craft, physical education are all provided as a matter of course with laboratory or workshop or practical facilities, but by tradition music is not. It is only a handful of progressive and far-sighted authorities that have developed any equivalent practical facilities in the way of music rooms, practice rooms, schools of music, youth orchestras, and so on. Overall, there is undoubtedly a shortage of music teachers of vision and imagination. What then of the follow-through op-portunities? I would say this is very difficult indeed in most areas of the country. Where there are no youth orchestras or choirs, where music and dance seem to be the poor relation, it is obvious that youth workers who have an interest or personal proficiency in some aspect of the subject ought to exert pressure on the authorities to improve the facilities in schools. A good deal more advantage ought to be taken of the E.F.D.S.'s facilities—they have always been the well-head of folk music provision in this country.

I have quite arbitrarily picked out physical activities and music as examples of secondary school subjects which lend themselves to follow-up after school. There are obviously others. Drama at first sight appears to be both a difficult activity and one attractive to comparatively few young people. On the other hand, it is an activity which demands the participation of a wide age range of people and on the whole would be one which would bring together young people and adults. Equally it is an activity in which participation by academic children is as important as participation by the rest, for the former's preoccupation with mainly abstract studies makes the practical balancing experience of drama all the more important. The development of film-making and photography, the fine arts, sculpture, and wood carving depend a great deal on the availability of reasonable practical facilities for their development.

On the other hand, the attractive development of other subjects and facilities which are commonly provided in secondary schools can be tackled perfectly successfully. For example, the library service, (witness our "Books for Enjoyment" experiment in Leicestershire), can and should be used far more fully by Youth Service than it is. Poetry and literature and modern languages all provide platforms in the secondary schools from which to spring forward. In connection with modern languages, I would like to quote again from our local experiments in Leicestershire over the last 2 or 3 years. Basing our thinking on the increasingly wider development of modern language teaching in schools via the oral approach from the primary schools upwards, and on the increasing amount of foreign travel by young people especially via the youth hostel movement and the like, we have organized or are proposing to organize, a series of days in France, Germany, Italy, Spain, Russia and Scotland. These take place on Saturdays, starting at 10.30 a.m. and going on to 5.30 p.m. You do not have to speak the language all the time (even if you can!) and this is clearly stated; but if you wish, native or fluent local speakers are on hand, staff from the embassy of the country concerned talk and lead discussion, national songs and dances are arranged, a film is shown, slides of customs and family life might be flashed onto the screen, a meal is served typical of the country illustrated, and its wines and its cigarettes are available to those who want them. These ventures are entirely self supporting, the ambience created is remarkable, and young and old alike participate in an unusual and stimulating experience. Ingenious treatments of such subjects are limitless.

There are a number of other important aspects of secondary

education which are worth considering by youth workers who wish to understand the potential bases for co-operation and for the development of wider activities for young people once they have left school. Not least of these would be a study of school societies and clubs. Very often the continuance of activities developed in these depends on the personality of the teacher and on the facilities, if any, available in the district in adult organizations. There is undoubtedly scope for school societies and clubs to offer "taster" opportunities for young people so that they can discover in their last year or so at school, a natural interest and be encouraged to pursue it at a higher level after leaving. In this connection, school societies could involve specialists and outside bodies like the Y.H.A., Y.F.C., Red Cross, parents, of course, and the minority skills of the teachers themselves. Youth workers are not generally aware of the development of self-programming groups in some secondary schools and of the increasing numbers of sixth form centres, fourth and fifth form social areas, especially in the developing comprehensive schools, with all this means for the nurturing of self-discipline, personal responsibility and a more informal approach to education based on a learning situation rather than on a largely direct teaching situation. An important new concept stimulated by the Schools Council and the Nuffield Foundation is that of the new teachers' and development centres springing up in the areas of many authorities. These may be primarily provided for curriculum regeneration at all levels and for preparation for raising the school-leaving age in particular, but they must surely from their very inception have youth organizers and workers in on their management and use. These centres could well be the power-houses for creating lines between schools and Youth Service, for here teachers and youth workers can come together in discussion and practical groups, can examine each others ideas, develop new materials and approaches, and interchange and modify techniques developed with success in their respective spheres.

The values of counselling and pastoral care especially in the comprehensive school are rapidly beginning to be appreciated more and more in secondary schools. In Leicestershire, we already have half-a-dozen or so teachers who have followed, or are following one

year supplementary courses in counselling at the University of Reading. This relates to the whole question of careers preparation in schools. In this connection, I have already referred to the various schemes now being developed in different parts of the country for the introduction of large numbers of teachers to industry and its opportunities. Again, what steps are taken by Y.E.O.'s careers and other staff in secondary schools to advise on the availability of after-school further education and Youth Service opportunities in the locality, and to what degree are parents brought in on this? Of course, quite a number of young people are involved in junior youth organizations, in the Duke of Edinburgh Award and in junior community service long before they leave school; but it still remains true that the majority are not and the majority probably do not consciously associate Youth Service and adult education as offering follow-through outlets for interests developed whilst at school.

I want to end with some assessment and description of the value of the joint appointment of the youth leader/tutor in forging more closely the relationship between schools and Youth Service. I select this subject because it is about the only consciously developed method of breaking down isolation between these two areas which cater for this common age group of young people between 14 and 20; and of increasing professional understanding of their respective functions and problems, and deliberately involving in a number of cases the young person in his or her local community in the fullest sense. There are a number of significant factors in these developments which I want to enumerate: (1) they are to be found exclusively in the L.E.A. sector; (2) they are generally associated with youth/school appointments for communities where the existing school or college buildings have formed a base for extension by youth and adult facilities; (3) they very often serve integrated community provision for a district, e.g. the village and the community colleges; (4) they thus often operate in school/college, youth/adult building complexes unlikely to be equalled in a community provision sense in the present climate of capital expenditure; (5) their sort of approach ensures that purpose-designed and built plant allied to the greatest amount of practical and recreational premises and playing fields in a district, are used to their maximum and most economical capacity throughout most of the year; (6) they generally ensure that the youth worker is able to get in touch with young people in an informal situation before they leave school, and can introduce them to the club premises by actually using them for normal school periods; (7) they are in constant daily contact in the staff room with all teachers having to do with the young person from 11 years upwards. The effects of youth work approaches and techniques seen at work both in the day and evening on a secondary school campus are probably some of the most healthy and organic means whereby the school curriculum will be loosened up; (8) in many such situations adult education provision is also on hand as well as youth work provision. Once again, the youth joint appointment may well have its counterpart in the adult joint appointment. In this situation, there can be free interchange of specialist facilities and tutors for young people and adults alike. Where all the components of school, youth and adult wings are integrated yet insulated from each other, there develops a natural movement between the youth and adult wings. Many young people take evening classes of a vocational or non-vocational nature, and after 9.0 p.m. very often gravitate towards the club; meanwhile in the 8.0 p.m. break between classes they often go to the adult common room for refreshment with the other class members; (9) the joint appointment in the village and community college situation probably has the best opportunity of doing something tangible towards bridging the inter-generational gap and obliterating the appalling adult rejection of youth or rather adult ignorance of young people through simply not taking the trouble to get to know them and their moves; (10) such appointments find themselves in the cultural and recreative power-house of the local community, and very often in situations of self-government and in control of independent financial resources going far beyond the usual pattern of independent youth clubs. The community provision of the village/community college type ensures the continuance of the democratic self-programming process right through from the secondary school stage. Indeed, if the latter has tended to be somewhat rigid and didactic, then the processes of college council, management and programming committees, election of youth wing members on to the youth management committee and the like, with the unfettered right to charge a college membership fee and also take a fee from voluntary societies and clubs who use the premises which they can then use for their own purposes without any public audit, has resulted in a breaking down of rigidity all round and an efflorescence of the learning process.

Not enough is yet known of the infinite variety of joint appointments in existence up and down the country today. One thing is quite certain, that in themselves they are extremely flexible. Many speak as if a joint appointment is of the one type only, namely the youth tutor teacher, but nothing could be farther from the case. Neither do they operate solely in premises linked physically to a secondary school. Some have the very loosest connection with other educational establishments, and are considerably separated from them in terms of distance. Others are independent agents as far as their youth work element is concerned, and so on. I am not saying that joint appointments are the only way of staffing Youth Service, but I am saying that there is a far greater chance of generating an interesting and healthy progression from school into Youth Service and further education if both the latter are served by some joint appointments. They are in on the ground floor as it were, they command unrivalled facilities and equipment and they are generally firmly rooted in a real community provision and concept. Young people can see and mix with adults off duty, and the latter much more readily accept young people when they see they will not bite them and when they can study their strange gear at first hand.

As I said at the outset, youth building programmes providing mainly free standing and independent premises, especially in the voluntary organizations sphere, have been a necessary rescue operation. Now let us hope that provision for youth, deriving from an enlightened learning situation in the associated common secondary school, will be consciously geared into the community provision for a neighbourhood in such a way as to provide each element with insulation without isolation. This will take many forms and will never be standardized; indeed, the example of Withywood has probably caused more standardization of open planning than was ever dreamt of, and many who now operate in such premises are far from happy with them. I hope that we will all demand a much more global approach to the school and community needs of individual districts, in the future planning of new building extensions and adaptations for schools, young people, and adult education. When all is said and done, we could not do much worse than we do now in putting down penny packets of unco-ordinated educational and community buildings here, there and everywhere. No wonder our present ideas for a leisure service are so hopelessly disparate and need a bit of educational and social magnetism to pull them together.

REFERENCES

1. E. PHILLIPS, *The Role of the School in a Changing Society*, Goldsmiths College, 1965.
2. CENTRAL ADVISORY COUNCIL (England), 15 to 18 H.M.S.O., 1959.
3. BOARD OF EDUCATION, *Service of Youth*, (Circular 1486), H.M.S.O., 1939.
4. MINISTRY OF EDUCATION, *The Youth Service in England and Wales*, H.M.S.O., 1960.

CHAPTER 5

Youth Service as a Part of Further Education

R. D. SALTER DAVIES

YOUTH SERVICE was invented in 1939, in the early months of the war; there had been plenty of youth work going on before, it now needed co-ordinating and organizing. The same government that decided the Youth Service should exist decided that it should exist within the education system—it was as simple as that. "Youth Welfare" said Circular 1486 in announcing the Youth Service, "must take its place as a recognized province of education, side by side with Elementary, Secondary and Technical Education."[1] There is an old world flavour in the vocabulary; the Board of Education, while quite sure that the service has a place in education, is still not quite sure what that place is.

By 1943, the White Paper on Educational Reconstruction, that prepared the way for the 1944 Act, was rather more precise in its language.[2] Youth Service "should take its place as an integral part of the national system of education". "Integral part" is a bit firmer than "recognised province" but what has become much firmer is the concept of the national system of education in which the Youth Service is to take its place. "The Government", said the White Paper, "propose to recast the national education service. The new layout is based on the recognition of the principle that education is a continuous process conducted in successive stages." Elsewhere the White Paper says that "the measure of the effectiveness of earlier education is the extent to which in some form or other it is continued voluntarily in after life".

This conception of education as a process continuing through life was finally embodied in Section 7 of the Education Act of 1944. [3]

> The statutory system of public education shall be organized in three successive stages to be known as primary, secondary and further education; and it shall be the duty of the local education authority for every area, so far as their powers extend, to contribute towards the spiritual, moral, mental and physical development of the community by securing that efficient education throughout those stages shall be available to meet the needs of the population of their area.

These are magnificent words. It is my personal belief that in spite of the immense improvements and developments since the war in schools, technical and higher education, we are still an immense distance from achieving that noble declaration of intent.

Elsewhere the Act makes it tolerably clear that the place of the Youth Service is in further education. Section 41, the first section in the part of the Act headed "Further Education", lays down the general duties of local education authorities with respect to further education, and includes among them that of securing adequate provision for leisure-time occupation in cultural training and recreative activities. It is a little unfortunate that Section 53, which prescribes more specifically the duty of local education authorities for securing adequate facilities for recreation and social and physical training, and on which authorities rely for their Youth Service expenditure in particular, should be in a part of the Act headed "Miscellaneous Provisions" and follows immediately on sections dealing with the provision of milk and meals and of clothing in maintained schools. But since the Act, the department and authorities have acted on the assumption that the Youth Service is a part of further education.

I must also call attention to another provision of the Act: the Minister of Education was empowered to appoint a day from which all young people not in full-time education should be obliged to attend part-time further education for one day a week (or its equivalent) and their employers should be compelled to release them. The Youth Service was to be the complement to a system of county colleges, and for a very few years after the war, the expectation that county colleges were only just round the corner had a profound effect on the development of the Youth Service in many areas.

The Youth Service became a part of further education then, almost as the result of the rationalization, after the event, of administrative action undertaken in an emergency. The important consequence is that the Youth Service is primarily a service for normal young people, a natural complement and continuation of their educational experience in schools and colleges, and only secondarily is it a service for the handicapped, the deprived or the depraved.

Some regret this bitterly and accuse the Youth Service of choosing the easier job of tending the sheep who are saved and neglecting the lost sheep, the proportion of whom is much larger than the 1 per cent of the parable. I myself am under intermittent pressure from admirable and passionate social reformers who want me to turn the Youth Service into a service primarily for social rescue and reclamation, to use my influence on the colleges of education to turn themselves into agencies for the training of social workers to work with young people in social need and moral danger. I sympathize; indeed I recognize that the Youth Service has a strong therapeutic function in relation to normal young people, as I shall show later, and is also in an unobtrusive way attempting much more than formerly to bring the socially alienated into a happier relation with society. But the intentions of the Act, with the additional glosses of the White Paper that preceded it, seem to me absolutely clear; the Youth Service is a normal part of the educational system and this is the policy within which the Secretary of State and his officers, the local education authorities and the voluntary organizations have to work, with whatever liberality of interpretation.

Things might easily have gone the other way. I have already spoken of the Youth Service as having been constituted in its present form by administrative action in an emergency. Circular 1486, issued in November 1939, from which I have already quoted, commented on the lack of provision for the social and physical development of young people between the ages of 14 and 20 and went on: "War emphasizes this defect in our social services; today the black-out, the strain of war and the disorganization of family life have created conditions which constitute a serious menace to youth." Thus the immediate motive for setting up the Youth Service we now have was social rescue, although its purposes soon become much wider and Circular 1516 seven months later took a very different line.[4] So too, the great wave of voluntary youth work in the last century was inspired by the need for social rescue; universities and public schools established missions in Slumland, the Girls Friendly Society cared for the morals of young housemaids living away from their homes, the Boys Brigade was an answer to juvenile gangs in Glasgow. But all of these have over the years found wider, more creative and more constructive purposes.

The first consequence, therefore, of establishing the Youth Service in the framework of further education was to determine its major function as the continued education of normal young people. The second consequence, was to put the local education authorities into a position of considerable power, if they cared to take the chance. A few did not and still do not; most took their new responsibilities seriously and a few of them over-seriously. Some authorities, including very influential ones, in their anxiety to play fair with the voluntary organizations and to avoid duplicating the work of the organizations, saw their own contribution to the Youth Service as the provision of youth centres of a kind the voluntary movements could not and would not want to undertake —a revival of the pre-war junior evening institute. Some thought of the Youth Service as a preparation for the county colleges soon to come and reached out to grasp the spectral fingers of the county college. Some introduced a principle of quasi-compulsion; every member must undertake at least one serious activity a week; every club or youth group must be able to show a programme of serious activity if it was to be registered with the authority and qualify for the authority's aid. (I have known barbola work and painting daisies on innocent glass tumblers get by as serious activities.) Compulsion could not be absolute: the member could always walk out, the youth group could refuse aid on those terms. But it did amount to the imposition of conditions stricter than the situation called for.

I appreciate the authorities' difficulties. As the Albemarle Report said, "learning is what the public will expect from the Youth Service, if they are to contribute to its cost". The authority have to make it manifest that its Youth Service does provide opportunity for learning. The chief education officer of a northern county borough got the chairman of his education committee to read the Albemarle Report when it first came out; the chairman flung the report on the chief education officer's desk a few days later and said: "This Report makes out the Youth Service to be fun. Well, we aren't going to pay for fun." Even when an educational situation is naturally enjoyable, we are sometimes impelled to inject something unpleasant into it simply to prove to the public that it is not being asked to pay for fun.

I am not, of course, arguing that activities are not good—far from it. Nor that some activities are best learned through attending classes. Nor indeed that an authority or a voluntary trust may not be fully justified in providing centres for certain specific learning purposes and in making them available only to young people anxious to learn them. But I do say that the principles and practices I have described were too dominant in the Youth Service for some years and are still too dominant in some areas now. These practices can produce very good work of its kind, but where they are over-dominant they tend to limit the exploitation of the full educational opportunities of the Youth Service. They limit the service in the following ways:

First, they over-emphasize one kind of learning—the learning of activity and skill—at the expense of other kinds of learning which may be more important for many young people: the learning, through experience, of making choices, taking decisions, accepting responsibility, organizing what they want to do in the way they want to do it. Second, they over-emphasize the class as the only sort of learning group. The class is a good medium for learning some things, quite unsuitable for others, and the full opportunities of learning may in fact be frustrated if the group has to tie itself to the rusty old framework of a class structure. Third, a Youth Service dominated by these practices tends to go on treating young adults as children. It does not speak to what is adult in the adolescent. It does not satisfy his need for self-determination. Fourth, a service on these lines tends to offer too little satisfaction to the social needs of young people.

For, let us remember, few of the young people who take advantage of what the Youth Service has to offer think of it as "an integral part of the national system of education". Admittedly some join an organization, a club or a centre specifically to learn; it may be first aid or home nursing in the Red Cross or St. John's Ambulance cadets, the life and work of the countryside in a young farmers' club, sailing or rock climbing, music or theatre in a specialist or general-purpose activity centre. But most young people join a youth club for sociability. Nevertheless the wish to do something, to undertake an activity, can and usually does emerge in a reasonably happy social situation. "They won't want to sit drinking coffee all the time", Lady Albemarle has said—perhaps a trifle optimistically. Even if they do, good social experience, as I hope to show later, can have considerable educative value. I believe the Albemarle Report to be right in saying of the young: "Their social needs must be met before their needs for training and formal instruction." I would compare the provision of the Youth Service in an area to that of the students' union of a good college of further education or college of education: opportunities for association, with the minimum of conditions necessary for the preservation of person and property, but with the opportunity of committing yourself, if you wish and only if you wish, to a wide variety of activities, physical, cultural, religious, scientific. The Youth Service being what it is, these opportunities will seldom be provided in one building; but the complex of groups in an area, within easy reach of a youngster's home should, in a fully developed Youth Service, offer this range of choice. And the fewer strings attached the better; the adolescent needs to be treated, as the Newsom Report argued, as the young adult which in effect he is.

The motives of the youth worker therefore are often very different from those of his clients. It is in the general-purpose club or centre that there arises most often this divergence of interest between the worker and his members, with the worker anxious to exploit in this situation the educational potential of which the members may be unaware. Before we consider what that educational potential can be, I should like to say as a matter of personal dogma, with which I know many experienced youth workers disagree, that youth work is most likely to succeed where the worker acts on the assumption that his first task is to give his members what they want—whatever else he can help them to find which they did not originally expect. The Youth Service will flourish in so far as it earns the reputation of a happy service, in which the young can meet each other and learn to find themselves and each other without being organized along ways they do not particularly want to go. But it should also be a service which offers, to those who wish, rich opportunities to commit themselves.

On the educational potential of youth work I would make three points. First, that it does not exist only in the activities which can be promoted. It exists also in the natural association of young people, in which, as the Albemarle Report said, they "may maintain and develop, in the face of a disparate society, their sense of fellowship, of mutual respect and tolerance". To turn their association to full account the adult working with the young needs something at least of the understanding proper to social group work. Some acquire this by training and experience. Some have it only by natural aptitude and experience and are barely conscious of what sort of talent they are exercising. One of the main purposes of training both of full-time and part-time youth workers is to help them to understand what they are doing and, because they understand, to be more effective in future. Where the worker does understand what he is doing, he is trying, quite deliberately, to use young people's experience in a group to help them to form happy personal relationships among themselves and with others outside the group; and his purpose is to influence the development of individuals and of the group to their own benefit and to the ultimate benefit of society.

My second point is that the educational value of activity does not lie only in the standards achieved. These are, of course, important; an individual youngster is immensely enriched by the experience of performance at a high level; the experience may affect him for life. But activities are also the context within which personalities interact. That is why I have been critical earlier of the sort of youth centre (there were many, there still are some) which separates activity and association: the greater part of the evening is given to activities organized in classes under instructors, with the consolation that the last 40 minutes will be given to association. This is to miss an opportunity. I am not arguing that classes have not a place and an important one. But I see particular virtue in the more informal group which can be helped to make its needs explicit, to see the range of possible action, to decide as a group on the course to be followed, to accept responsibility for organizing what they want to do to the utmost of their power and still to see where they will need help, advice and training and to accept that need. This seems to me to be good educational experience which can continue and enlarge the work of secondary schools in helping young people to grow up into responsible citizens capable of making their own informed decisions. The concept in the Albemarle Report of the self-programming group has much in common with the concept in the Newsom Report that secondary pupils should be made to feel that they are partners in their own education.

My third point is very much a tertiary one but perhaps not without importance. Activity being generally a means to a further end, we should judge the value of activity by its value to the individual, and not according to some absolute scale of academic hierarchies, with intelligent theatre and music at the top and darts and popular dance at the bottom. Activities in youth groups often appear trivial. But a young man who has not been particularly successful at school, who is engaged in trivial, repetitive work in his employment, may find his club the one place where he can be himself and may, in a session of popular dance, reach the top of his form when he has never before been top of his form in any other sense. A group of young people badly estranged from society may be brought by a sympathetic worker to undertake the clearing and redecoration of the damp and dusty basement in which they meet; this all sounds trivial and nugatory but the fact that they can co-operate at all on a job of minor utility may be a minor triumph, a sign that they have changed course.

To me, in short, the educational value of youth work is to enable adolescents, through successful group experience, to learn more of themselves and of their fellows and to find out the kind of adults they would wish to be. It is essentially a process of self-identification —of identity search—and of self-determination. In this the Youth Service continues the work of good secondary schools and—I hate to say this—makes good what indifferent schools have failed to do.

For, as I said earlier, the Youth Service has a therapeutic and remedial function not only with footloose groups out in the social Badlands but with numbers of apparently normal young people. It is difficult to say this without appearing to reflect unfairly on the secondary schools. It takes a man of my age to recognize fully the immense improvement there has been in the education of the adolescent in schools and colleges in the last third of a century. There are hundreds of secondary schools in the country as successful in personal relationships as in their teaching. It remains true that there are still numbers of pupils leaving school thankfully, resentful and dissatisfied with their school experience, eager to get to work, and often finding disappointment in their employment. They may be nearly full-grown physically and personally underdeveloped. The Newsom Report quotes some evidence on the personal quality of some recent school leavers of average or less than average ability; one piece of evidence runs:

> We feel bound to record our opinion that many of these less gifted young people are socially maladroit, ill at ease in personal relationships, unduly self-regarding and insensitive; their contact even with their peers if often ineffectual; they understandably resent being organized by adults but show little gift for organizing themselves.

Young people like this exist in not inconsiderable numbers and their existence is some justification for the emphasis that the Youth Service now puts on personality and the interaction of personality. The kind of experience offered them in the Youth Service is a kind that they should and could have had at school and which is indeed offered in hundreds of good schools, where (to quote the Newsom

Report again) "pupils take a hand in their own education so that they feel that they are being treated not only as real people but also, what is even more important, as people who have the capacity to form a right opinion". Although there is much in common between the objectives of the good youth worker and the good secondary school teacher, the Youth Service does not yet command the full respect of secondary school teachers who feel that what they try to achieve through a demanding curriculum the youth worker attempts through recreation. It is worth recalling one more quotation from the Albemarle Report: "Recreation can be as educative to the adolescent as play is to the infant and as influential in promoting the development necessary to turn the teenager into a responsible adult."

There seem to me two other forms of educational work with which youth work has much in common. First, work in colleges of further education, particularly the local colleges mainly concerned with the education of 15- to 19-year-olds. I have spoken earlier of the flourishing students' union, with its complex of students' societies, as a good working model of what an area Youth Service might be. I feel on principle that there ought to be a much closer relation between the Youth Service and these extra-curricular activities of colleges of further education. But there is also much within the curriculum of colleges of further education which has similar purposes to those of the Youth Service and between which and the Youth Service there ought to be a closer link. I speak of the work done by liberal studies and general education departments of colleges of further education with young technicians, craftsmen and operatives. Some of this work is much more like the work of a good youth centre than employers care for; they complain that they release their young employees to college to enable them to become better workers, not to follow hobbies, like music, art and the crafts. I know of areas where the colleges effectively realize their function in relation to the community; they serve not only their own full-time and part-time students but also other young people of the same age in the area. But these efforts are still sporadic and I believe there is a big field of development here.

Another area of quasi-educational work with features very similar to those of youth work is community development; indeed I believe youth work to be a special application of community development. By community development I do not mean only the work of community centre wardens; that too is a special application of community development. The term community development is not well understood in educational circles in this country; it is assumed to be an appropriate form of aid to be offered by highly developed countries like ours to the emergent countries; but it is not commonly thought necessary in well-to-do industrialized countries like those of Western Europe with comprehensive welfare services. I believe that community development is badly needed also in industrialized and complex societies, which are precisely the societies in which the population is increasingly on the move, socially and geographically and in their employment, and in which therefore the traditional ties of neighbourhood and community and craft are greatly weakened. What the community worker tries to do is to encourage groups of people, and individuals within the group, to exercise their initiative, take decisions and accept responsibility, without in any way undermining their autonomy or making them dependent upon him. When he is in touch with a group, he is concerned to help them to identify their needs and to make them explicit. He will feed them with information and give them access to information that will enable them to see what courses of action are possible within their resources; he will bring them to the point of decision but will not take sides himself and must leave decision to them even at the risk that they will decide unwisely.

This is very similar to the function, as I described it earlier, of the youth worker as a social group worker. This is how the community centre warden works in relation to the complex of voluntary groups and societies affiliated to his community association. The field of application is much wider than education in the narrower sense. New town corporations understand the need for this work if the new communities they are bringing into being are to have a vitality of their own, and they employ teams of social development officers (under various titles) to do just this sort of work. Some housing managers and members of their staff in the employment of housing authorities, have shown remarkable aptitude for this work. Secretaries of rural community councils and councils of social service need these skills; so too, I should imagine, do parish priests and other clergy working with groups of adults.

But there is also a direct application of this process to educational work, and not only in the Youth Service or community centre work. The full-time principal of an institute of further education or evening institute will find many educative voluntary societies in his area (local history societies, field study societies, language circles, science clubs) whom he will wish to serve and help and whose independent initiative he will try to maintain. The adult tutor in a community college in Leicestershire will be in the same position; so is the head of a department in a technical college responsible for the non-vocational further education of adults; so is a tutor–organizer of the W.E.A. All these are likely to be more effective with voluntary groups of an educational kind if they understand and try to apply the processes of community work as I have outlined them. Nor are these processes irrelevant to the work of the Head of a primary or secondary school, if, as the Newsom and Plowden Reports both urged, the school is to influence the community and if the understanding of the community is to enrich the life and work of the school.

I suggest, then, that youth work has some elements in common with teaching in school, teaching in further education and community development. I suggest further that this recognition ought to affect our systems of training. Here I must emphasize again that what I say is a personal view, the view of some of my colleagues and me, and is not departmental policy. And my colleagues and I have no developed plan; I am simply scribbling aloud. I would like to see an ecumenical movement in further education, an intercommunion between professional workers in the various branches of further education, youth service, teaching in colleges of further education, community work, adult education. I would like to see a state of affairs in which a person entering further education, after initial training, as a young man or woman or as a mature adult, took it for granted that he would be changing from one field of further education to another three or four times in his professional life, improving, I hope, his professional standing in the process and gaining in wisdom from the variety of experience. The way to get to this situation, I suggest, is to recognize the value of *sandwich training* as we have experience of it in further education. Sandwich training involves at least two periods of academic training and further or higher education with a substantial period of paid employment in between, under supervision both by the training agency and by the employing agency. The final period of academic training should enable the student to digest, rationalize and turn to account what he has learnt in his period of paid, supervised employment.

The system already exists in the training of teachers for work in colleges of further education. It has its advocates as an appropriate system for the training of primary and secondary teachers. It has, for example, been urged that what is now the teacher's probationary year should be officially incorporated in the training pattern, to be followed by a further period in college through which the student could draw together the results of his experience. We could couple with sandwich training the rather different conception of professional training by stages, a system which, I believe, will be forced on us by two facts of life; that women will insist on training for professional work (not only in education) and also insist on getting married soon after or even before they have completed their professional training. It is a commonplace that the life-cycle of women has changed in the last 20 years; they marry much earlier, bear children earlier, control the period of child-bearing, and are ready for full-time professional work from the age of 35 onwards. If we devised from scratch a system of higher education and professional training to meet this changed pattern of life, we would provide a short period of initial training leading to an intermediate qualification and entitling them to practice their profession at least part-time, followed much later by a further period of professional training through which they could become fully qualified. The colleges of education are used to providing shortened courses for mature students; I commend to their attention the need for shortened courses for immature students as well. What is an appropriate pattern for many women could become a pattern for some men; they could undertake relatively short basic training, entitling them to work as qualified practitioners in certain fields, with the possibility, recognized by them from the start, that, if they have the wish and the capacity, they could take further training, end-on or after some years, that would widen their professional scope.

If we can get a relation, recognizable from the start by the incoming student, between training for Youth Service, community work, and some forms at least of adult education; if we can add to that a bridge, also recognizable from the start and to be crossed by a further period of shortened training between work in the youth and community field and work in further education establishments and in schools, we shall have broken down the present professional isolation of the youth and community worker. And the Youth Service is too much isolated. As I have spoken of the Youth Service as a part of further education, you will have realized that its place is still anomalous; it has taken its place alongside other forms of education, as Circular 1486 said it should, but it still remains curiously unattached. Many authorities have attempted to attach it to the schools, with good results often, with deplorable results sometimes. A few have attempted to attach it to colleges of further education and I believe this is well worth further exploration. A few have attempted to attach their Youth Service both to schools and to the adult education carried on in the same building, but by and large Youth Service is still very much on its own.

One result has been an uneconomic use of capital resources. Professional associations of youth workers and voluntary youth organisations have protested about the niggardliness of capital allocations for Youth Service building—this is only human. And yet the Youth Service should recognize that in the whole field of non-vocational further education, involving millions of adults and young people, only one service spends more than the Youth Service. That is sport. Local projects for the amateur pursuit of the arts can get limited grant from the Arts Council. Adult education and community work, for which I care just as much as I do for the

Youth Service, have only meagre trickles in comparison; there is no building programme. The Youth Service, in contrast, has been far better treated. Nearly thirty million pounds worth of capital resources has been committed to it since 1960. This puts on the Youth Service a heavy responsibility for making sure that it uses its capital allocations to the fullest effect, particularly at a time like the present when there has been talk of cuts in educational expenditure. Much of our capital expenditure has gone on buildings which are used only for four hours a day, sometimes only for three nights a week. And yet we in the Youth Service have long complained about the under-use of other educational buildings, secondary schools in particular, for community purposes.

We have reached a stage of development in which we should be consciously trying, so far as we can, to link the Youth Service with the stages of education which precede it, which run parallel with it and which lead on from it: with secondary, vocational and adult education. Authorities which maintain separate youth centres based on a structure of formal classes might well question the need for special provision of this kind if they already have a flourishing system of adult centres or institutes of further education. We may have been too cautious about developing youth work in community centres. The link between the Youth Service and the corporate activities of colleges of further education is much weaker than it could be. Single interest youth groups may be all the more effective if they are affiliated to voluntary adult societies with the same interest. The young should be encouraged to use arts centres and sports centres, and the centres should be planned with this use in mind. Indeed the Youth Service may be brought into happier relation with other forms of educational, cultural and recreative provision by effective multipurpose planning—that is, by the planning of educational and non-educational buildings for community use.

But at the present time, I do not believe this to be the whole answer; there seldom is only one answer to any educational problem. It is argued that there is in this age, a gap between adults and adolescents as has never existed before, and both Professor Mays and Professor Marsh discuss this elsewhere in this volume. My personal view is that adolescents differ as much from each other as they do from adults; that many adolescents are more influenced by adult values than by those of their own age group; that many others react against adult standards, thinkingly or unthinkingly, and have no wish to consort with adults. Where a gulf exists, we shall not bridge it by pretending it is not there; and I see no escape from the necessity for making some separate provision for youth for years to come. Meanwhile the more effectively we can relate youth work with comparable forms of cultural and social provision, the more successfully we shall realise its essential purposes.

REFERENCES

1. BOARD OF EDUCATION, *Service by Youth*, (Circular 1486), H.M.S.O., 1939.
2. MINISTRY OF EDUCATION, *Educational Reconstruction*, (Cmnd. 6458), H.M.S.O., 1943.
3. *Education Act, 1944*, H.M.S.O.
4. BOARD OF EDUCATION, *The Challenge of Youth*, (Circular 1516), H.M.S.O., 1940.
5. CENTRAL ADVISORY COUNCIL for Education (England). *Half Our Future*, ('Newsom Report'), H.M.S.O., 1963.
6. MINISTRY OF EDUCATION, *The Youth Service in England and Wales*, H.M.S.O., 1960.

CHAPTER 6

Probation Service and its Relationship to Youth Service

Frank Dawtry

In my preparation of this paper, I have consulted a cross-section of probation officers in all parts of the country. In doing so I have concluded that the views and experiences of officers vary so much that none could be representative. I can therefore only offer a collation of observations about the relationship between the probation service and Youth Service. I am sure that there is, and must continue to be, much collaboration between the two services—we are all in the same job in the long run, and probation officers should know the local services and youth leaders should know the probation officers. It is obvious, yet it does not always happen.

The term "Youth Service", of course, covers a variety of organizations, but the main point of contact between the two services seems to come with membership of youth clubs by probationers, or use of probation by members who get into trouble.

I thought at first that it might be simple to summarize some of the views I gathered, and I asked many of my colleagues what, from their experience, was the relationship between the probation and youth services. Here is a typical reply:

> Some youth clubs I would not touch with a barge pole, and I would certainly not recommend my probationers to attend them. Others, of course, I would be only too anxious to get my lads interested in. The one thing which has always been clear to me is that the strength of any organization depends upon its leader, and no matter what accomodation or equipment is provided for a club, it will fail if it has not got an imaginative and enthusiastic leader. So far as my relationship as a probation

72

officer with the Youth Service is concerned, this has depended completely on my experience of the leader of the individual club. In some cases I have a very close working relationship with a club leader, because I have had respect for his abilities and confidence in his maturity and judgement. In other cases, experience has led me to have only a superficial relationship with a leader, because I have not been able to have much confidence in him!

Next, from a very young woman officer who would, I thought, be very keen on contacts useful to her teenage girls.

I hardly know what the Youth Service is.

A senior probation officer in the south:

In suitable cases we invoke the aid of youth leaders to accept clients a members of their clubs and centres, and where special attention is necessary, we have discussed this with the wardens and found that, with few exceptions, they have been prepared to cater for these special needs.

From another officer, in a nearby area:

One meets and chats with members of the Youth Service at local social workers' gatherings, but rarely does one have any dealings with them at work. Occasionally a youth club leader will telephone to complain about a probationer who had been misbehaving in his club, but this does not usually develop into a constructive case discussion.

A northern officer:

In an earlier appointment I maintained close contact with Local Authority youth club leaders who would take lads on probation, introduce them to the clubs and keep a special eye on them. Now, I maintain contact not only with Local Authority club leaders, but with voluntary bodies.

From a large city:

... although from time to time clubs have been approached, they have given little help and there has been little effort on the part of the club leaders to recruit from the ranks of the delinquent.

A principal probation officer in a city:

Another matter which is emphasized by most youth leaders in my experience is that they are not in business to deal with delinquent boys and girls, they are there to cater for the ordinary club member. "Ordinary" appears to mean the member who is not seriously disturbed or delinquent, and one can sympathize with the view that the club can cope only with a very limited number of emotionally disturbed or delinquent members.

A woman officer:

> I have had good help from the better youth clubs, whose leaders have "rolled their sleeves up" to help; but I could count on one hand the number of youngsters on probation who have become permanent members of a youth club. Most clubs are too sophisticated for our youngsters demanding a high standard of conduct or attainment which probationers feel unable to achieve. They are capable of it, but they do not think that they are.

An experienced senior officer in the midlands:

> Although I have been a part-time club leader and hold a national certificate in youth leadership, my offer to help the local youth service, to serve on any committee on which I could be useful, to help in any activity, has never been taken up although repeated to more than one youth organiser. The professional youth leaders do not want probation officers too closely identified with their work and their clubs.

These then, are a sample of the views of probation officers about Youth Service. What do youth officers think about probation officers and their work? In a pamphlet "*For young people—service in your neighbourhood*", Alec Dickson says that "Probation officers are reluctant to share their responsibility with others"; and at a recent conference in the north, one youth leader expressed the view (apparently shared by colleagues) that " . . . it is the job of the youth leader to protect the underprivileged against the coldness of bureaucratic social workers". Other members of the conference expressed strong feelings about the probation service; some envied its strengths, but there was much criticism of it for its aloofness and condescension towards youth workers. A county youth organiser expressed his view at another conference that there was little contact between the probation service and Youth Service because the Youth Service was too respectable to appeal to the usual run of probationers. A probation officer who has been in both services commented;

> There is a great gap between Probation Service and Youth Service; unfortunately this appears to be the fault of the Probation Service, and in consequence the relationship is rather haphazard. From my own experience, both as a leader of youth clubs and now as a probation officer, I feel that the probation officer tends to get bogged-down about confidentiality which, although it has to be observed, seems to erect an insurmountable barrier. This is a pity.

A woman officer told me:

> For some years, while at university, I lived in a Settlement and took a practical interest in its youth club, but I never came across a probation officer. We met clergy and voluntary social workers, but not probation officers.

Isolation, co-operation, respectability, aloofness? There is evidence of all of these, but I have found good examples of co-operation in practical activity. A Principal Officer told me that in his area there is good co-operation, although this is not extensive, while within the same area, a senior officer told me that with few exceptions, leaders have been prepared to accept probationers and cater for their special needs.

> An ex-borstal boy with a very disturbed background was given special consideration, despite his very difficult behaviour at a centre, and eventually responded so well that he went with other members on visits abroad. Another lad with outstanding feelings of inadequacy was encouraged by a centre warden, who made opportunities for him to be in positions of responsibility, and eventually the lad was elected as a members' committee chairman.

In one city the probation hostel was turned into a club, and all boys in residence are members, with much support from local clubs, the hostel club winning many trophies.

Another officer commented:

> The clubs vary in their set-up and amenities, but one feature seems to be common: in an area where parental interest is poor the club leaders seem to act as substitute parents. They provide for some of their members a personal support not found at home, and thus do a valuable piece of work.

Certainly there is plenty of evidence of a desire to work together;

> I have always welcomed the opportunity to get together with youth leaders either on an individual or group basis.

> While pressure of work often precludes this, I believe that there should be much more contact and co-operation between leaders in Youth Service and probation officers. Often one does not know of the others' interest in a particular young person. If there were to be closer liaison and informal meetings, then this barrier would be considerably reduced and much information could be exchanged to the benefit of the young person in question.

> In B . . . a probation officer is a member of the Youth Service committee on unattached work and discusses problems which youth leaders encounter in their daily work; this is a form of case conference and has possibilities.

This leads me to ask whether we can expect these two services to get closer together? It is part of the larger problem now being discussed by social workers, in the Standing Conference of Organizations of Social Workers, and perhaps in the Seebohm Committee.* Should there be a comprehensive service or association of these engaged in social work, on the grounds that everything we do has a common basis? Or should there be a federal organization within which the specializations might be preserved? Or should the specializations continue in clearly differentiated organizations which can collaborate at appropriate points? My own experience is that while it is obvious that some needs remain unmet, our present untidy organization with its admittedly wasteful overlapping does mean that a lot of people do find the place where they can best be helped, and that a variety of sources of help is a good thing for them. I think that this applies to youth work as to any other service.

Is it true that the Youth Service or the Probation Service take an isolationist view of their work? I am convinced that any closer co-operation between these two services can develop only by day-to-day work in the field. A wise probation officer will not hesitate to call on the help of a club leader or youth organizer; and a wise club leader will similarly not hesitate to seek the advice of a probation officer or to consult him about some member of a club who seems to be drifting, or about a known delinquent member who seems to

*Written before the publication of the Seebohm Report, 1968 (Eds.).

be getting into new difficulties. Much is being done and can be done between the two services at this level, but no one can compel a response. We have no right to expect club leaders to accept probationers and then have the probation officer come round every week to see how the lad or girl is getting on. If the club leader is asked to help, there must be some mutual trust and some divestment of responsibility to the leader, who must feel that he has this trust and is sharing a responsibility. It is not unreasonable that a probation officer should seek to use clubs and other youth services, for he is charged with the responsibility of making the best use of all available resources on behalf of his client; but as one youth leader said in my enquiries: "If I am to be asked to take the lot—to fill my club with probationers—I might as well become a probation officer."

Apart from individual help by mutual agreement, however, we must ask whether the Youth Service should be expected to deal with delinquent youth. The suggestion that some youth leaders are too respectable, or that they do not want to be associated with probation officers or probationers, may be true, but it may be unfair to criticize them on this account. Some youth clubs want to get on with the job of providing a service for young people who might drift; others for young people who are in no danger of drifting, but who need a common meeting place to carry out their mutual concerns, which may include schemes for the welfare of their community. It is easy to understand the reservations of a leader who fears the contamination of the damaged apple in the barrel and has to consider his responsibility to his other members. In some cases the leader and club members have been willing to take a probationer, but the parents of members have objected and the leader has been faced with a serious loss of membership.

There is also evidence that the willingness of youth organizations or club leaders to help with probationers may be diminished by the unwillingness of probation officers to take them into their confidence. This word *confidentiality* came up time and time again in my inquiries, yet, as one of my colleagues said; "Leaders feel that they should be informed if a member is on probation; this could certainly be helpful, but one needs to know one's youth leader and his attitudes before entrusting him with personal information." Another probation officer commenting about the problem of confidentiality said:

> The youth leader is fully aware of the problems of confidentiality. In most cases, particularly with a professional leader, he will have his terms of confidence well and truly defined. Quite often the club leader will know as much about a boy or girl and the family as does the probation officer, if not more, for on the whole he sees far more of the boy or girl at the youth club than a probation officer does in the artificial environment of an office, and in many cases the club leader also visits the home.

However, a Principal Probation Officer puts the matter like this:

> It has been difficult to get across to these workers (youth leaders) that if a boy and his parents are unwilling for the probation officer to bring the matter to the notice of the club leader there may be difficulties. I say there may be difficulties, because once a relationship of mutual trust has been established between an individual probation officer and an individual club leader confidentiality may not matter much. I have turned this question back to youth leaders by saying "Suppose a boy in your club talks to you about a personal problem and emphasizes its confidential nature, would you tell the probation officer about it?" It is at this point that understanding seems to grow.

This is it. We all have our responsibilities to respect confidence, but on the other hand, in professional relationships one of the bases must be a willingness to exchange confidences knowing that these will be respected. This is accepted between professional social workers. This leads me to the next point for discussion. Do youth leaders regard themselves, or do they wish to be regarded as social workers? Is their link with the educational world one which makes them see themselves as primarily responsible for a form of continuing education for those who wish for this? Or do they now see that their role might be that of a social worker, since they cannot fail to become involved in the problems and anxieties of an age group which is rarely deviod of these?

In a Parliamentary debate last March, Mr. Crawshaw, M.P. (Liverpool, Toxteth) asked if our youth services had the right objectives. One of their purposes he said:

> is to keep people out of trouble, or to help them to do so, *but that is not their main purpose*. The type of person who gets into the criminal courts

is not the type who normally gets into a youth club and it's that fact that worries me. We are spending considerable amounts of money, yet do not seem to be touching the fringe of this class of people whom the youth clubs *should primarily be serving* [my italics].

He seems to be saying that what is not their main purpose, should be their primary purpose. In replying, Mr. Denis Howell (Minister with special responsibility for Youth) said that the Youth Service was not a first-aid service, a net to catch all those who may be falling from society: "It is much more positive than that . . . it is concerned with the development of the whole personality of individuals in our society . . . ."

That seems to me an excellent description also of the job of the probation officer with those who come into his care, and if he can find help in the development of that whole personality through the Youth Service or in a youth club, he should do so, and here will be a demonstration in action of a unity of purpose. Mr. Fred Jarvis, in the recent symposium *Trends in the Services for Youth*,[1] puts this well. He interprets the probation officer's role as being,

> To help the delinquent to come to terms with the demands of society and to relate acceptably to institutions and to its individual members, and to conform to their reasonable expectations. In practical terms, he encourages his younger probationers to attend school regularly, to join appropriate youth organizations, to make proper use of the youth employment service, to work regularly and industriously, and at the same time he does what he can to interpret his probationers' behaviour to the school, the youth club, the employer, so that he may be better understood and helped [Mr. Jarvis admits, nevertheless] . . . that most of society's institutions are designed to meet the needs of the normal non-deviant person, and it is for this reason that schools, youth clubs, etc., reject their delinquent members after certain limits have been reached; their behaviour can be tolerated so far, but when the interests of the organization or its members appear to be endangered then their toleration diminishes.

This is a fair summary, and it only underlines my general belief that what is needed is plenty of opportunity for members of both services to meet and understand their respective problems. This demands a willingness from both parties and there can be sceptical members in each service. It means a willingness on the part of

Youth Service to help where it is reasonable to do so; but an equal willingness on the part of probation officers to realize that the word *reasonable* must mean what it says. Dealing with delinquent and disturbed individuals is a specialist job—probation officers have constantly, and rightly, made this clear. There can, therefore, be no complaint when the youth leader says "this is as far as I can go in the interests of the rest of my members", for he, too, has his special responsibility.

Nevertheless, there may be, and have been, plenty of examples of active co-operation in which youth leaders or probation officers have left the close confines of their jobs. *The Times* recently said, "The Home Office might stimulate the Probation Service to experiment more with the use of young volunteers in relation to juvenile delinquents within their care", and the current development of the use of voluntary workers and organizations in after-care may well lead to calls for this sort of service. We already have evidence of this. We have cases of borstal boys being taken to camp with youths from clubs; girls on probation being taken on a holiday tour with a club. "A local youth club have had young prisoners working in their community projects and they are beginning to play their part in our after-care scheme", one officer told me. Another said, "A local youth club warden has been taking an interest in the incidence of drug taking in the area and has been liaising with probation officers on this problem. There is scope here for some collaboration." Probation officers can be equally helpful to club leaders and I have just been told of an interesting experiment in a quite large probation area, covering two or three Boroughs, where one officer has been appointed liaison officer with the Youth Service and an effort is being made to provide a consultative service where youth club leaders can contact the probation officer regarding problem members:

> They sometimes mention the names of the people concerned, but this is entirely up to the individual leader. It is possible to assist the leader to deal with a situation rather in the way a tutor officer assists his student. On a field level, the scheme has worked well enough, although only with a limited number of clubs and organizations.

He adds that in one part of the area the scheme has been completely ignored by the Youth Service, no letters have been acknowledged and "so far as they are concerned the scheme might as well be a well kept secret". The result of this liaison has been very valuable to both sides; one club has "adopted" an approved school, taken a party to the school, and had a joint sports day and now seems likely to develop joint camps. Another club has taken a high percentage of boys from detention centres and borstal, and the leader is very concerned about these lads and their particular problems.

In other areas I was told of instances of something more than co-operation, amounting almost to a pooling of activity and a blurring of the line between the two services. One or two probation officers have turned their offices for a night a week into a temporary youth club and have had the help of youth leaders in this. The development of group work in probation has in some cases only been possible with the help of a youth leader who is better trained for this than the probation officer.

The opportunities for a trained youth leader and a probation officer to collaborate in this way with a delinquent group are obvious; but from one area the opinion was given that probation officers might first pave the way:

> Delinquents can be led into the activities the community provides, including the Youth Service, by the extension of group activities within the probation setting. By this means, the non-clubbable type can learn to be more sociable and to accept the variabilities of human relationships— and then introduced into a club.

I go on to refer to training as an area in which greater contact may, or should lead to greater understanding. I found little official contact here, but many local examples of probation officers taking part in local training schemes.

> I have been used regularly for lecturing at training courses for youth leaders, and my services have been enlisted by my appointment as a member of a house committee at the youth centre.

> I have talked to youth leaders when they have been attending an area course, and youth leaders in this area have always been able to visit us or attend juvenile court when necessary.

I have given an occasional lecture to youth leaders, and one of my colleagues has recently been asked to include two lectures in a youth leaders' course, organised by the county.

One officer informs me that the full-time youth leadership courses in his area always include a lecture on delinquency. A principal probation officer suggests that the inadequacy of training causes some concern to youth leaders and feels that perhaps a period of attachment to a probation office during training would be a great help. Another principal probation officer from an area quite near the training centre in the midlands says that they have only once been asked to take a student from the college.

On the other hand, there seems to be a very serious lack in probation training of any information about the Youth Service. Several of my informants have no recollection of any lecture or discussion about this during their training, and only one or two had any contact with local youth services even during their period of practical placement with a probation officer. This seems to be a serious omission, but I am told that in fact a high proportion of the younger entrants to the service have taken part in youth work of one sort or another before coming into training.

What can we do about it? Are we all too busy to find the time to meet, or are our training schedules too tight? It seems to be of great importance that youth workers should have first hand knowledge of the probation service if only because many of them must come to the age when they feel it necessary or wise to give up youth work, and when their valuable experience of youth work and of varying family backgrounds and difficulties may well make them excellent candidates for the Probation Service which is now encouraging the recruitment of mature entrants.

I find considerable co-operation at fieldwork level, perhaps less at the higher levels and even less at national level; but I do not think that any great national get together will make any difference. We all need more time to sit back and look at our fellow workers; we all need to learn that none of us can solve all the problems alone, although this is a difficult lesson for any social worker to accept. I am sure that on a one to-one basis there is a lot of goodwill and active working together, and this applies between all the social work services. I believe that there are personal difficulties, "empire preservers" and clashes of temperament, but these too are to be found within the same service and will not be eliminated by any top-level policy-making bodies. But I do believe that there could be much more sharing of experience in *training*; and that the inclusion of some basic understanding of each other's job and responsibility and aims and purpose at that basic level when we are all receptive, could make for more mutual understanding and co-operation in our fieldwork.

I am not anxious for more organization. I can see no nice tidy solutions—I have seen many of them tried, but I have also seen that it is not necessary to regard everything as a problem, and always to be spending time seeking solutions. It is often better just to get on with our own job and meet our fellow workers when and as necessary. I have never been a believer in too much organization, ideas bring into being organizations, which then often proceed to smother the ideas. I think that round-table conferences and large national committees give us a good day off in London now and again, but if they lead to more permanent organizations they may also involve Parkinson's law. I do not believe in ideas like "one big union", or in these great umbrellas people talk about—for who is to carry the umbrella, and what if we do not all want to go the same way home? I do believe in the innate common sense of *most* social workers, and I see no better solution to the problems of co-operation than to rely on that.

REFERENCES

1. J. H. LEICESTER and W. A. J. FARNDALE (Eds.), *Trends in the Services for Youth*, Pergamon, 1967.

CHAPTER 7

Youth Employment Service and Its Relationship to Youth Service

HERBERT HEGINBOTHAM

THE appearance, in the *Times Educational Supplement* of 7 July 1967 of an advertisement by Essex County Council for a Principal Youth Employment Officer, which referred to the Youth Employment Service as "formerly integrated with the Youth Service", reminded me that the two services might be said to have a common origin in the after-care movement of late Victorian and early Edwardian times. This is particularly true in Birmingham where it was the Central Care Committee—already by 1910 encouraging out-of-school activities of various kinds, which took up the new choice of employment work allowed under the Education Act of that year. The "youth work" side expanded rapidly in 1916 as the juvenile organizations Committees were set up. It further expanded locally through play centres (1917) and camp schools (1920 onwards). The Central Care Committee had a broad concern for the general welfare of boys and girls as they left school, many as young as 12 years of age. So we find the different strands of employment, further education classes and opportunities for leisure-time pursuits, all being roved together to form an ever stronger educational and social life-line for the young. As time has gone on, these strands have themselves grown into separate, though interlinked, supporting systems.

84

THE YOUTH EMPLOYMENT SERVICE

I should like to spend a little time making sure we are up to date about the Youth Employment Service. Historically, one of the great compelling reasons why enlightened local education authorities fought for the privilege of running this service was that their vision of it was of a broader, educational–social service of advice and help than the rather narrower job-finding, job-filling, concept of the Labour Exchange of 1909. This is shown clearly in the scheme published by Dame Ogilvie Gordon of Aberdeen in those early days.

The objects of such a service have been defined as "To assist the individual to choose, prepare for, enter upon and progress in an occupation". But definitions are subject to the interpretation put upon them by those who do the work. So we find in many areas that there has been insistence by the youth employment officers themselves on the duty of the service to make known to young people opportunities in further education, and for leisure activities. Equally the opportunity has been seized to bring before employers the importance of their contribution to the development of the young person. Two main avenues of approach can be seen. One has been the attack on straightforward exploitation so starkly revealed in the national and local reports on "boy life and labour" of Edwardian times. The other is propaganda in favour of better selection, better training and better manpower development. A new problem —equal opportunity in employment for racial minorities—is being resolutely tackled by the service.

The service also has a duty to the school and college system. Living as it does by continuously collecting information about occupations, training opportunities and about young people, the service has sought to persuade schools and public opinion, firstly, that the vocational implications of educational choices should be taken into account when optional courses are chosen in secondary schools. This follows from the conclusion reported in the Birmingham researches that educational and vocational guidance are part of the same process. And, secondly, that adequate attention should be given to the preparation of young people for their change of status from pupil to young worker (or to students in an adult institution). Some current criticisms of the Youth Employment Service may indeed reflect the success of its efforts to gain acceptance for these ideas.

But the ramifications of the basic work itself are often not fully understood. May I remind you briefly. A careers service is many sided, and involves:

(i) Careers information for pupils and parents. This has to be collected, verified, published and circulated. In 1966–7 we circulated in Birmingham 21,168 copies of 143 publications to 173 schools and 17 colleges. Eight *new* titles were added nationally to the *Choice of Careers* series, which by now numbers well over 100 titles. Information must be promulgated by group and visual methods as well as in written form—a formidable undertaking for an age group numbering about 15,000. It is a matter of organization, hard work and the harnessing of voluntary effort to mount the annual careers weeks with about 200 speakers and chairmen.

(ii) Each youngster's needs are unique, so many more than 15,000 individual interviews are held annually in Birmingham, mostly at school. For these, facts about capacities and aptitudes must be collected by our partners, the teachers, and by the youth employment officers. These have to be evaluated in the light of the pupil's views of his needs and inclinations and of his parents' wishes. The advantages and opportunities in further full-time education are as much in the adviser's mind as occupations. A careers adviser cannot function effectively without an almost encyclopaedic knowledge of both careers and courses.

For those interested in counselling techniques let me assure you that we have been client-centred as long as I can remember. By this I mean that we have and are using both directive and non–directive methods. As Hackman wrote in James Adams' *Counselling and Guidance: A Summary View*[1], both counselling and guidance "can be client-centred . . .

we need both". So the approach must be eclectic—inspiration and horizon-widening for some, for others a strong lead because their need for this is not met in any other way. Some depend upon the youth employment officer's ability to think clearly through their situation and suggest a good line of action; others only need to be shown the method and will quickly solve their own personal equation. "Finding oneself" in terms of work is an intensely individual matter in which youth employment officers know they can help, but not dominate. The choice of career is one of life's major problems, and because of this, family conflict and dissension occassionally come to a head in the interview situation, requiring great tact.

(iii) The *placing* service and the *advisory* services were conceived by the local education authorities as corollaries one of another. For Birmingham, this means recording the notification of about 25,000 vacancies every year; checking them and classifying them so that they are available for immediate and continuous reference, and so that when action to find a job is promised something really happens. Our placing activities result in the issue of about 30,000 introductions to employers each year.

(iv) "Follow-up" or "after-care"—or "review of progress". No longer is there a small army of voluntary after-care visitors calling on young people; postal invitations to attend the bureau are the most common method. But in some areas (not much in Birmingham) youth employment officers invite attendance at a local club or centre. Sometimes they just drop in to the club and are available for inquiries or just conversation.

I spoke earlier of the need to involve the schools more in the preparation of pupils for employment. In addition to supplying material for schools, careers libraries and helping to build up the knowledge of careers masters, it is logical that the Youth Employment Service should be bringing teachers, youth employment officers and employers together by means of short conferences, "introduction to industry" courses and work experience courses. This is an "open-ended" area of work which is limited only by the staffing capacity of all three groups.

RELATIONSHIP WITH THE YOUTH SERVICE
IN THE FIELD

I have already referred to the youth employment officer's sense of the importance of the contribution of leisure-time activities (including clubs and other pursuits) to the development of the individual's personal qualities. This is for its own sake, but the vocational incentive can be used in the interview situation in furtherance of this objective. When I was in Oldham just after the war, I used to pass on to the youth organizer, details of any requests from youngsters for pursuits which were not available and quite a few useful new departures began in this way. In other cases clubs gained new recruits. I still believe this to be a most important type of liaison.

Some of my Birmingham colleagues used to visit evening institutes regularly to make contact with the young people outside working hours, and did valuable work not only in helping individuals through moments of stress at work, but in keeping in touch with the changes in values and attitudes. Recently I assigned some of the Birmingham Assistant Organizers to visit a large central club because of rumours that members attending during the day were unemployed but were not coming to the bureau. Although this particular hypothesis fell down on examination, club members' employment problems do arise. What can a leader do?

The first thing is to listen. Many problems solve themselves as we talk to a sympathetic listener who makes non-committal but encouraging noises. Equally important is to know your youth employment officer. I mean personally. Visit him or her. Talk with him and get him to show you his bureau and to talk about his work. Get the youth employment officer to visit your club and see your work—and problems. Out of this may come a new line of approach to a youngster, or a different view of a manager or foreman. A leader who establishes such a relationship will be able to recommend a member to go and see—not "the youth employment officer"—but a named friend who is known in the club.

Such a leader will realize the amount of knowledge, both individual and general, which is required before a particular career can properly be recommended and will not, therefore, be tempted to give such detailed advice. But he *will* be able to encourage his members to believe in choosing careers by rational means, which is what the Youth Employment Service stands for, of course. Friendship with and confidence in the youth employment officer will rub off the leader on to the member, at least for the first time. After that the youth employment officer is on his own. Above all, helping the member to discover himself, whether he is patient, or sociable or whatever other quality he is unsure about, is perhaps part of the purpose of the Youth Service. It is certainly a great help to anyone in deciding their career.

Counselling those in work to learn to adjust to foremen and workmates is always worthwhile, but siding with them "agin the government" rarely is. Influence with both sides is lost because usually neither side is wholly blameless. Finding out the facts is often therapeutic but frequently best left to the proper agency. The youth employment officer will know which this is if it is not obvious. Too close involvement may end in the leader losing his potential influence as the "honest broker", able to effect adjustment or reconciliation.

I have known leaders put on careers evenings. But employers can be very angry about anything which appears to poach their scarce supplies of young workers, and this is understandable. On the whole I think this inadvisable and should *never* be done without the complete agreement of the youth employment officer.

There is a wide field of work for teachers and for the Youth Service in promoting general adjustment to life, including working life. Much interesting work along these lines is being done in Birmingham and neighbouring areas. Formally organized courses have been organized by the National Association of Boys' Clubs for many years, and locally a joint body representing voluntary organizations is developing additional facilities.

As you can see, my view as to the proper relationship in the field is one of co-operation based upon a personal relationship and a proper respect for each other's professionalism. Many youth employment officers who are also part-time youth leaders have at one time or another expressed similar views. It follows, then, that I believe in the value of fraternals, social workers' luncheons and other occasions when youth leaders and youth employment officers can get together. If only we all had more time!

THE RELATIONSHIP AT TRAINING LEVEL

At least one obvious and elementary need is met when arrangements are made for students in training for both services to learn about the companion service. We should go on from this to think of these words of Sir Lionel Russell's to the Institute of Education Summer School of 1961:

> For myself I should like to see some large-scale experiments with some new type of Colleges of Professional Education, in which future teachers could learn and mix and play with future entrants to many other professions, particularly those covered by the general term of social work and those concerned with some of the arts.

This suggestion is particularly important for the Youth Service because the McNair Report in 1944 hints,[2] and the Jackson Report of 1949 states,[3] that "many people believe that there is not a lifetime's career in youth leadership". I have therefore tried to compare the entry and training arrangements of the two services. First as to age: both seem agreed that 23 is a preferred minimum age at which to begin practising. In both cases, staff shortages force a relaxation of this, but the Youth Employment Service will not allow full professional duties to be assumed under 21 years of age. As to entry qualifications, there is some difference. For youth leaders five O-levels; for youth employment officers, unless they are definitely mature candidates, a qualification of degree or H.N.D. standard is needed for entry to training, together, if possible, with work experience outside the guidance field. The need for the latter is obvious. Length of training for youth employment officers is one year. Youth leader training may be one or two years.

The subjects studied have some common elements but one must beware of misleading descriptions. Psychology probably means different things to youth employment officers and to youth leaders. The former needs much knowledge about aptitudes and abilities as well as adolescent characteristics; the latter perhaps less about aptitudes, etc., and more about emotional development and group dynamics. Both groups study social institutions but for different purposes, and their study of educational systems has differing, as well as common, objectives.

Subjects studied in depth by youth employment officers but not by youth leaders include the structure and organization of industry, and the study of employments. Their involvement in practising individual interviewing technique is also considerable. Group work is studied too, for the purpose of holding discussions and passing on information. Youth leaders probably do more of this and less of individual interviewing. Each studies the structure and running of their own service.

While informality is a very strong aspect of youth work, the very fact of having to deal with each individual as an individual, and to deal with the business of job-filling and job-finding brings its own sense of structure into the atmosphere of a bureau. The youth employment officer adopts the minimum of formality in manner and speech, but displays a common sense acceptance of the frame of reference associated with the concept of work undertaken for wages. Though a youth employment officer must cultivate detachment to survive, he cannot escape concern for "his leavers". Detachment and involvement are important to many youth leaders also.

The detail of the youth employment officer's job, for which his training must prepare him, includes the rules about school-leaving, about working hours, national insurance and so on. The correspondence, the urgency of daily action on vacancies and the increase of tempo as end of term approaches, all add to the pressure. Then there is the very large amount of work with adults: parents, teachers, foremen, personnel officers, including some of great seniority, and many others. I sometimes think we deal with adults almost as much as young people.

I have never been a youth leader, but my inquiries lead me to think that one of its satisfactions is the freedom in the job to invent and change methods and approaches. While great freedom exists, too, in the Birmingham Youth Employment Service, the nature of the work as I have said, imposes its own discipline. Professional people influence their professions, but the reverse is true too, and some youth leaders' temperaments might be more and some less able to adapt to a change to the more detailed, structured, atmosphere of the Youth Employment Service.

Nevertheless, youth leaders who seek at the right moment to become youth employment officers will be those who have sufficient intellectual ability to absorb quickly the mass of information needed, personal maturity and a capacity for dealing with much detailed business efficiently and quickly while retaining the human touch. Such transfers would be much more frequent probably if, in the future, Sir Lionel Russell's suggestion were to be taken seriously and an attempt made to find the highest common measure of subject content for all professions making an attempt "to contribute towards the spiritual, moral, mental and physical development of the community . . .". Assuming that joint courses would take students mainly between the ages of 18 and 20, not all youth employment officers would be trained this way, since we need many who have direct experience of open employment of every conceivable kind; but I am sure such courses would provide recruits of a most valuable kind, especially if they came to the Youth Employment Service after a few years in one of the companion services such as the Youth Service.

CONCLUSION

In their book *Adolescents and Morality*, the Eppels wrote:

> . . . perhaps the real challenge of young people today . . . is the challenge to our capacity to come to terms with change in human life . . . Young people are constantly before us as a reminder of the impermanence of many things.[4]

The speed of change is so rapid nowadays that every youngster is entering a new world. He or she is in a sense opening up new frontiers, and every new age group renews this experience. Since all beliefs and customs are being questioned and reformulated or discarded to an extent probably never equalled since the days of Aristotle, the sensation of wide-openness associated with frontier life is accentuated. In such a setting the only proper relationship for our two services is that of the partnership of true friends.

REFERENCES

1. J. F. ADAMS, *Counselling and Guidance: A Summary View*, Collier-Macmillan, 1965.
2. BOARD OF EDUCATION, *Teachers and Youth Leaders* (McNair Report), H.M.S.O., 1944.
3. MINISTRY OF EDUCATION, *Recruitment, Training and Conditions of Service of Youth Leaders and Community Centre Wardens* (Jackson Report), H.M.S.O., 1949.
4. E. and M. EPPEL, *Adolescents and Morality*, Routledge and Kegan Paul, 1966, p. 223.

PART THREE

YOUTH SERVICE, SOCIAL WORK AND INTERPROFESSIONAL DEVELOPMENT

This final section considers the changing pattern of voluntary youth work (a major element in the contemporary Youth Service), and reviews the rapidly developing structure of social casework training and practice. Relationships between these two professional areas are taken up, and broader inter-professional implications are then developed in more detail in the final two papers.

CHAPTER 8

The Future Contribution of
Voluntary Youth Organizations

LESLEY SEWELL

IT MIGHT be possible to divide an audience of this kind into those personally committed and passionately convinced of the permanent and splendid role of voluntary organizations, those—a vast majority—prepared to accept that some of them, at some time, and under proper supervision, are useful and do a good job; and a small group, extremely doubtful whether voluntary organizations are more than an excrescence on the Youth Service and should be dispensed with at the earliest possible date.

In any case, I am grateful for the opportunity after nine months of retirement to be encouraged to think again on this subject. I have found it useful and interesting, but I would make it clear at the start that I lay no claim to any kind of prophetic inspiration. This is no more than an attempt, on the basis of experience, to make some assessment.

The primary question is essentially simple, and is perennial. What is there in the experience and roles of the voluntary youth organizations which, in the setting of the 1970's, will be worth preserving and worth fighting for, and what is, or will shortly become, just dead wood? Further, what are the new functions, if any, which should fall to their lot? To understand these issues and find the action to take are presumably the reasons for including this topic in the conference programme.

First, briefly, one or two negative propositions. I would certainly not attempt to look ahead on any long term or semi-permanent basis. The Youth Service is still in process of formation, Heaven forbid that it should ever be anything else. In dealing with this age group, the acceptance of any mould, however good, and attempts to lay down blueprints or to state infallible doctrines are surely the ultimate heresies. We are not concerned to stress past splendours or to list the contributions made by the voluntary youth organizations —that extraordinarily heterogeneous group. These contributions are well-known and, by and large, accepted.

Nor are we concerned to compare or to grade the contributions made by the various organizations. In a conference on inter-professionalism it may be relevant, in relation to the Youth Service, to point out how much fruitless time has often been expended on arguing the relative contributions of education and social work or the relative merits of a teacher or a caseworker in the Youth Service field. Both are essential; each brings its special contribution. It is surely equally true that the various youth organizations have made their own individual contributions, of a wide variety, and are not to be measured against each other.

If, for the moment, the past can be taken as the pre-1940 era, clearly the voluntary organizations—then in almost sole possession of the field—had a pioneering role on a considerable scale. Pioneers of remarkable stature were thrown up in almost every organization. People like Baden-Powell and Stanley Smith in the early days, Basil Henriques and Josephine McCallister Brew a little later, come immediately to mind; individuals of an independence of mind, a quality of character and personality, and perhaps not infrequently, some element of the fanatic. It is worth remembering that while each of these, and others of a similar calibre, contributed in no small measure to launching or developing particular youth organizations, their main contribution lay in the fact that they were individuals deeply and continuously concerned about young people, and part-icularly underprivileged young people; individuals not only able to make remarkable contacts with boys and girls but also able to fire other men and women with something of their own enthusiasm.

Perhaps we look back occasionally, with some nostalgia, to the comparatively simple aims of youth workers of those early days.

Their motives were straightforward and charitable—a concern for the welfare and education of poor and underprivileged children. The workers, almost entirely voluntary, were motivated by a deep and sincere religious faith and concerned with providing the elements of the good life.

What about the next stage of development, the present and the more recent past, which have seen a pattern of incredible expansion and development with almost equally incredible frustration and stale-mate; which have seen attempts to assess the Youth Service, to give it a new look, to transmit a new content, or from time to time to fight a rearguard and defensive action? It must be noted that even in these years of rapidly increasing statutory provision, it is frequently the voluntary organizations who have pioneered the new developments. Take a subject of interest and universal concern at the moment—community service by the young. Voluntary Service Overseas, Community Service Volunteers, Task Force, International Voluntary Service and others, are each the outcome of individuals launching a voluntary movement. Or, take work with the unattached, that word so widely used and often with such confused connotation. It would be true to say that the pioneering work in this field has come largely from the voluntary organizations. The N.A.Y.C.'s Penguin,[1] the result of 3 years' hard labour, and recently the noteworthy textbook by George Goetschius and Joan Tash,[2] are two of many efforts in this field. Or again, the main developments in work with young people in industry—now part of the mainstream of many national youth organizations. (A recent figure of the number of boys and young men who had been through the N.A.B.C. Adjustment to Industry courses was eloquent tribute to the scale on which this has been carried out in one organization alone.) And finally, the many international opportunities, whether through the Boy Scouts' jamborees, the Y.M.C.A. and Y.W.C.A. international work, the N.A.Y.C. Greenland and Poland Expeditions or other less well-known but equally exciting ventures. These are clear testimony to the initiatives still held by many of the voluntary organizations and a look at what lies behind these may give us clues as to their future role.

Any time and motion study of the voluntary organizations' work would quickly reveal that money, the lack of it and the search for it, takes pretty considerable toll of the time, thought and effort of those most concerned, particularly at national, regional or county level. Is it equally true, if less obvious, that this concern with money has its own peculiar contribution to make? It would certainly be my experience that (while second to none in my dislike of this job), money raising is a way to create and maintain friends, and to secure their lasting interest and goodwill. One may grumble at the time devoted to this, but it remains true that not only may it have this positive and important result, it also acts as a healthy brake on some too grandiose schemes, when the brilliant new inspiration must be committed to paper and "sold" to the trust or other body holding the purse strings.

A personal example may illustrate that for many people this financial element is a deterrent to work with a voluntary organization. I had occasion last year to talk with two people who had worked with the National Association of Youth Clubs over a period and were considering their future careers. One of them said to me that she was determined to go into local authority service. On principle, as well as by temperament she could not consider any work where begging or money-raising was involved. A fair enough attitude, and good luck to her in the interesting appointment she has secured. The other, who had worked successfully during a number of years with a local authority before coming to the association, was equally clear that for her, a voluntary organization, whether N.A.Y.C. or another, offered the right opening for the future. Her comment, and main reason for this, was interesting. She had learned she said, a new relationship with her local employing committee, with the officers of this committee who had made her a friend and helped her through some quite serious personal problems; the basis of her relationship to her committee, of taking them into consultation, of expecting and securing their partnership, was something quite different from that which had been expected or given in a local authority set-up.

This, I suggest, is a second key to the role of the voluntary organization. Relationships of all kinds can be very different where ultimate responsibility to the rate-payers is replaced by this kind of partnership. The voluntary organization, at its best, is a close-knit partnership of senior members, leaders, staff, committees and honorary officers. The governing body represents all these groups, and policy must win their full support. The grass-roots cannot be ignored. There is no doubt that a fund of adult good-will towards young people exists today which can be channelled through a voluntary organization rightly operated. While much of it is available through statutory channels, some, for obvious reasons, is more readily obtained by a voluntary organization than a statutory authority.

The third role of the voluntary organization is to help young people and those concerned with them to live on a large map, to do things at a national and an international level. The international opportunities open to young people through their membership of the main voluntary youth organizations are today of a width and variety unknown in years past. Almost every association has its own international links, its own opportunities to put forward individuals or groups of young people for exchange visits, overseas scholarships, summer holidays or vacation experience. Conversely, most organizations are frequently concerned with young people from overseas wishing to participate in their conferences, their summer schools or their training courses. The residential centres owned by so many of the larger organizations provide the ideal location for such valuable contacts. Cross-fertilization of this personal nature is not only valuable in the international field. With the present *extraordinary* (and I use the word deliberately) variations in local education authority thinking and practice in the Youth Service, the role of the voluntary organization in making known something of the widely different development and experience in different parts of the United Kingdom, and in providing a kind of national observation service is a particularly important one. This divergence in L.E.A. provision means also that the function of "plugging the gaps" is not out of date.

Money, relationships, international links; what about the often more emphasized experimental role? Of course many local education authorities are today conducting exciting and valuable experiments, but two factors weight the scales against some of their efforts. In the first instance, experiment must mean possible failure. True experiments are bound to produce this share of failures as well as successes. Failures which are expensive to the rate-payer must not, like matrimony, be undertaken lightly. The local education authority cannot be responsible for expensive failures, nor for experiments which are on the razor edge of the wrong kind of notoriety. Secondly, experiments by and large, frequently depend on finding the rather unusual individual to carry them out. These people must often take risks in security, in the career structure, and must be left free to carry on with only the lightest of hands on the steering rein. Again, this is not easy for a statutory body, expected by most of its committees and councils to produce results or, at any rate, to avoid the wrong kind of press publicity.

This is one aspect of the freedom which, within a flexible framework, is of the essence of the right kind of voluntary organization. Take, for example, political freedom and religious freedom, both of great importance to the young: they do not lie as sometimes suggested, in a negative rejection or a refusal to become involved. If other young people are to be attracted and held, the political youth groups must become part of the Youth Service, and politics, not civics, must become a real part of activities and discussions. The religious approach must be equally positive. We need the committed people of all kinds, not hiding their beliefs but ready to play their part and to act in full and co-operative partnership with each other. These are not easy issues, but it is a field where the voluntary organizations, if ready to accept and welcome changes, have an obvious role.

All this should mean a constant reassessment of function. It is encouraging to note the various working parties which have over the last few years looked into a number of individual organizations —evidence that this need is taken seriously. We still have some way to go in making this process a continuing one. Two further aspects seem to me of vital importance. A national Youth Service is not, and can never be in the foreseeable future, equated with a national education service. This is the age-group which must have freedom of choice and must learn through its choices; the age-group which rightly joins and leaves its organizations, participates and throws away its opportunities, is politically flaming scarlet one day and bright blue the next, can be militantly agnostic at one moment and shortly after, the supporter of an Earls Court campaign. This is all part of the process of growing up. A wide range of choices offered by many different sponsoring bodies is a part of this learning process. We need variety—politically, denominationally, socially and programme-wise.

Secondly, however important the role of the qualified professional, or on however expanded a scale this is planned in the future, the youth service will continue to rely on what are from a trade union aspect, the professional "black-legs". It is as far as I know the only social or educational service which admits on a basis of equality, the volunteer and the professional. The youth leaders, the officers of units and organizations, have exactly the same role and responsibility as the full-time professional. This could not be true in the Probation Service or the Child Care Service, however much the professionals in these need to learn to use and co-operate with the voluntary helpers. The similar problem in the education service— the function and status of the teaching auxiliaries (or by whatever name they are known)—probably presents one of the biggest handicaps to the new look at schools and in the education service. The Youth Service will continue to depend not just on full-time leaders and paid staff, but on voluntary leaders of equal responsibility.

The formal educational services are increasingly aware of the need to form links in and with the local community. Many reports and speeches emphasize that if the school in the 1970's is to do its job well it cannot work in isolation. This is more obviously and immediately true in the Youth Service and the professional cannot do this alone. In *Razor Edge*,[3] that fascinating description of a youth club, the leaders—voluntary and full-time—came and went. It was Mrs. Blandy who provided continuity and contacts. There are hundreds of Mrs. Blandys, not so articulate and possibly not always so persevering, who are holding together the youth clubs and other units of the Youth Service all over the country. The role of the volunteers is a vital one, whether in relation to the professional leader or in their own right, as members of advisory and management committees, as participating in shared interests and specialist enthusiasms, as councillors, interpreters, and general helpers they fill an essential role. Perhaps also they help to prevent the Youth Service becoming one more hot-bed of unintelligible jargon and thus more remote from its customers, their parents, their employers, and their well-wishers.

Of course, many of these people are to be found in the so-called "statutory youth clubs", although it is rather more than just an impression that they are a diminishing number there as part-time payment has become so widely accepted. The civic youth centres in several of the larger cities have always relied on paid staff primarily recruited from the teaching profession. Whatever the reasons, the voluntary organization is often in a better position to recruit and hold on to the voluntary helpers and to offer them some share in a real responsibility.

May I elaborate this conception of the voluntary role by personal experience, not as ex-general secretary of a national voluntary youth organization but as chairman for the last eighteen months of the management committee of the local youth centre. Background: a county with a progressive and generous education authority, co-operating well with flourishing voluntary organizations. A small town (or large village) with a good record of community service, encouraged by the divisional youth officer to start a youth centre and offered the possibility of a redundant primary school with financial assistance towards a part-time leader. A committee set up the usual local mixture—the local county councillor, the clergy, an infant school headmistress, chairman of the parent/teacher association, a drama teacher from a secondary modern school and some willing housewives; the honorary secretary, a young man who had for some years been voluntary leader of a successful youth club, and a chairman press-ganged into the situation, as having at any rate heard of youth clubs.

What have the last 18 months shown as the prime jobs to be

done by volunteers? On *leadership:* advertising, interviewing and eventually appointing a part-time leader out of a very small choice who, within 6 weeks, was clearly not the right person. Then for a year, three leaders each running one evening a week, as the only possible way to keep the centre open. Finally, acceptance of the offer of a grant for a full-time leader from the county council followed by 6 months spent in advertising, interviewing, writing to training centres and one seemingly endless series of disappointments. (A full-time leader arrives in 3 weeks' time.) On the *building:* 11 months spent in obtaining a lease from the county council and the charitable trusts involved in some measure of control of the building. Personal visits by the county councillor and others to county hall; negotiations with builders, planning committees, plumbers, etc. All this without a typist or any secretarial help. Stamps, telephone calls, stationery and many other details can involve a great deal of time and money for the volunteer. *Membership:* the centre was largely taken over almost from the start by the least desirable and most difficult elements in the local community; rowdyism, damage, drinking, and a constant concern by the police and local residents.

What about the role of the volunteer? If I summarize briefly, the background can be left to the imagination:

(a) to recruit, encourage and keep happy some twenty volunteers who run the very attractive coffee bar which was installed, and to undertake numerous jobs;

(b) to deal with the horror expressed in various ways by a respectable suburban community at finding that within it there existed this law-breaking trouble-causing gang in considerable numbers;

(c) co-operation with and handling of the Press over many of the troubles that arose;

(d) meeting young members when the voluntary leaders or the part-time paid leader had reached a crisis point and taking action with the ring-leaders;

(e) endless discussions with the three leaders who did not see eye-to-eye on most things to do with youth work and had little previous experience;

(f) contacts, explanations and interpretations at all levels: it is worth noting that because of the power structure in this typical community, help is needed from people able to make these contacts at a variety of levels. No full-time professional could take them all over.

All this presents no unusual picture, but it is worth setting out as indicating the sort of role that even in a well-developed statutory and voluntary situation, still falls to the lot of the volunteer. What part did the Youth Service as such play? It was clear from the start that our local committee was nervous of the authorities representation, good as they were. Discussions tended to be inhibited in their presence. The local associations of youth clubs and boys' clubs were helpful but could not, in the form of a single staff representative for the whole county, cope with the kinds of details with which help was needed. Many volunteers have now been drawn into the circle and the centre can therefore claim to be in some degree a community effort, but we are under no delusions about the difficulties that still lie ahead.

Here is the "worm's eye view" of all this business about Youth Service. The V.I.P.'s in this service, administering, planning, thinking, lecturing, arguing, imparting knowledge of social group work, casework, community work, and many other things, should never forget the worms.

May I sum it up thus. Anyone concerned with the Youth Service is aware of changes ahead, of new patterns being hammered out, new ideas being tried and endless discussions taking place. What is to be the age range in future? Is the family the real unit? What is the connection with the schools? What is happening to the young adults? Should the service be community orientated, part of a total community? Or remain concerned with one group? Where should it be based? Is the conception of a club building no longer the right one? Is "programme" an out-dated word and even "activities" becoming slightly unfashionable? What is the picture of leadership in the future? How far can this be produced by training courses and training organizations? Where has "Bessey" led us?

Of course, all these are real and vital questions, not to be answered easily, and requiring to be worked out over a period of time. My thesis is simply this: the voluntary organizations have proved in recent years as well as in the past, that they can move forward and have an invaluable contribution to make if they are true to the main stream of their traditions and prepared, while clarifying their own aims, to make the necessary changes and then to continue to offer and be offered a real partnership with all other bodies concerned in the Youth Service.

REFERENCES

1. MARY MORSE, *The Unattached*, Pelican, 1965.
2. GEORGE GOETSCHIUS and JOAN TASH, *Working with Unattached Youth*, Routledge and Kegan Paul, 1967.
3. MARY BLANDY, *Razor Edge—The Study of a Youth Club*, Gollancz, 1967.

CHAPTER 9

Developments in Social Work Training

DAME EILEEN YOUNGHUSBAND

THERE is a great shortage of social workers at the present time. This may seem obvious, but it is a never-ending source of wonder to me when I look back to the days before the war when students completing the social science course at L.S.E. did not know whether or when they would get a job, when almoners, as they were called then, were out of work and the Institute of Almoners kept down the numbers they accepted for training in order not to have too many members unemployed. I remember, too, the excitement in the social science department when one of the students who had done particularly well on the course was appointed to a quite important post in a youth organisation in London at the colossal salary of £250 a year, against the normal £150–200. Even in the early 1950's the Home Office discontinued one of the university child care courses for lack of demand, and students with a child care qualification often found difficulty in getting an appointment when they finished their training.

What, then, has happened to change this picture so radically in the last 15–25 years? It is not easy to answer that question because attitude changes which are hard to measure have certainly played a very important part. It is true that the services which employ social workers have either come newly into existence or else have expanded very greatly since 1948. At the same time, the marriage rate for women has gone up, with the result that the turnover of women in employment is very much more rapid than it was in the days of those reliable spinsters about whom we made jokes when they were there but whose loss in the professions we now have cause to lament.

Looking back to the past, I would still say that the biggest change of all is the change of attitude among employing bodies who now take it for granted that they will try to recruit trained social workers if they can, and are indignant when these are not forthcoming in sufficient numbers. This is a far cry from the days I well remember when it was argued that older people educated in the "university of life" had far more to give than trained younger people. There was some element of truth in this before the recent developments in training. The earlier training was almost wholly a general education in the social sciences with some fieldwork that was really a kind of extended observational experience and a bit of apprenticeship training thrown in. In short, there was hardly any systematic attempt to enable the student to relate his theoretical studies to the world of practice. As Joan Matthews puts it in *Working with Youth Groups*: ". . . They had no opportunity to learn a method or professional discipline . . . . The lack of a professional method meant that the theoretical understanding they acquired could only be applied in a 'hit or miss' way, and for most of their practice they were thrown back largely on ingenuity and intuition."[1] Still less was it thought that the universities should make any consistent study of the real-life problems that faced social agencies. All this has changed out of all recognition with the development of planned professional training, and with far greater involvement by the universities in a type of social research which is concerned with urgent social problems like attitudes of tenants on new housing estates, delinquent neighbourhoods, unattached youth, or the social life of old people.

A good deal of the improvement in social work education was due in the earlier part of the 1950's to the help of American social work teachers who came here under the Fulbright programme and worked with British colleagues. They helped us translate their much more advanced and better thought-out methods of social work education into our own cultural terms so that the methods began to fit comfortably in this country. Of course, development of new methods also depended upon advances in the knowledge of human behaviour which made it possible to reinforce rather arid discussions of instinct, perception, memory and the like with an understanding of the dynamics of human behaviour in the common experiences of life. We needed this knowledge at what the Americans call middle-level abstraction, that is to say knowledge that makes it possible to formulate illuminating concepts which apply in a variety of circumstances and which are likely to be within the direct experience of students as they begin to practise in social agencies.

The Americans also helped us to move on from teaching the practice of social work by a series of anecdotes and illustrations: "I always found in my club that . . .", or, "I remember when . . .". The result was that in time we produced systematic case records which soundly illustrated certain generalizations about people's behaviour in various situations. For example we know that any form of major separation, whether it be through the loss of a loved person, through going to live in strange surroundings, through leaving school or home and starting a career among new people, leads to anxiety and to a greater or lesser extent to grief reactions. This is a natural process, but in its early stages the person concerned may be confused or withdrawn and may need plenty of opportunity to assimilate it by talking to a good listener. The general understanding of how people react when something happens that brings about a big change in their lives is insufficient in itself. Different people will react very differently according to their personality, their age and their life experience. Moreover, their responses, whether rigid or flexible, normal or pathological, will also be determined by their subcultural group with its accepted standards of thought and behaviour.

Parallel with these developments in a more precise and penetrating understanding of human behaviour, social workers here and elsewhere were trying to discover how this knowledge could be used to help people to cope better with the experiences that life or their own personalities thrust upon them. The focus has been on discovering how it would be possible to insert some kind of positive experience into negative situations, or to arrest or halt a process which might lead to permanent damage; or at least to discover how to "contain" a bad situation so that it might not get worse.

The primary tool of social workers is the use of a relationship between them themselves and those whom they seek to help. This means that the social worker must know how to make and sustain a relationship that can be used in different ways by different people according to their needs. Some, for instance, may need support and encouragement; others a permissive person who accepts them and gives them more realistic confidence in their own abilities so that they will neither shrink from life nor make hamfisted use of social skills. Others, who have very weak personalities, may sometimes need the support of an authoritarian relationship in which it is made clear to them which are the "halt" and which the "go ahead" signs.

I do not want for a moment to suggest that social workers have not always tried to understand people and to do things with and for them with the aid of other social services, the help of other professions and the use of material resources where these would help people to cope better with their troubles. What was new in the 1950's was that we began to learn how to do this much more systematically. This meant an orderly assessment of each actual case by applying knowledge about human behaviour and from our experience of using this knowledge, evolving a coherent method of practice.

We also began to teach through the use of case records which illustrated in fair detail the processes of interaction between the client and the social worker over a period of time, and showed through an analysis of what actually happened the kind of relationship and activity on the part of the social worker that was or was not helpful to different kinds of people. This use of case records is, as I have said, quite different from the earlier anecdotal period because the records are carefully selected to illustrate particular parts of the general theory and practice of social work. In the accepted pattern of current training, the course on this subject is closely interrelated with the parallel course on human growth and behaviour. The teaching also provides opportunity for much discussion by the students in order that they may bring in examples from their own practice and learn in the course of discussion to grasp and use new ideas.

So far, we have been more successful in relating concepts from psychology and psychiatry to social work practice than relevant concepts from sociology and social psychology. This is partly because these last two branches of the social sciences are still much more abstract than psychology and psychiatry. But all the same, a good beginning has been made and nowadays social workers are trained to take more account of social influences on individual behaviour than they were several years ago. Perhaps one of the reasons why sociology lags behind psychology in its application to social work practice is that sociology has not so-to-speak become *operational*, there is no practice of sociology as there is of psychiatry and clinical psychology. Nonetheless, students need to be fully conscious of the extent to which their own and other people's behaviour is moulded by social influences, for instance by accepted family and occupational roles, or by the attitudes and values of different strata or age groups in our society.

Earlier on I suggested that those people who thought there was not a great difference between the trained and the untrained were not altogether wrong at the time. I have referred to some of the ways in which knowledge from the behavioural sciences has been incorporated in social work practice, and the methods of classroom teaching we have evolved to make this come alive. But classroom teaching alone is only part of the story. Students cannot become real practitioners simply by talking. They must also begin to develop sufficient competence in applying the knowledge through practising the methods of social work with living people.

We used to send students to social agencies to get general experience. They might be passed from one worker to another, see all sides of the work, do a variety of things but never get any systematic teaching nor have responsibility for a caseload of their own. Almost the most revolutionary change which has taken place in the last few years has been the development of field teaching or supervision by social workers selected for the purpose on account of their qualifications, their experience and their interest in teaching students. The fieldwork is normally concurrent with the theoretical studies so that students may be able quickly to relate these to each other. Concurrent fieldwork also makes possible close ties between field teachers and the staff of the course. It is usual for supervisors to have regular meetings at the college or university running the course so that they can study the principles of field teaching and relate these to their own students.

Each student carries a small caseload for which he has responsibility. He records in detail the processes of the interviews between him and the client so that in discussions afterwards with the supervisor they may be able to understand better what was happening in the whole situation, what were the processes of interaction between him and the client, and what the student did or said that was helpful or not helpful to the particular person. This is also one of the means by which students are helped in the painful process of becoming more aware of themselves and other people. The student also has to face and come to terms with prejudices which he may not have suspected before about particular kinds of people and their behaviour. For instance, it is common for students to have strong feelings about the relations between parents and children and to take sides with one against the other. It requires a great deal of discipline and a certain amount of experience to learn that, very often, it is only by undertsanding and trying to be helpful to the "wicked" parent or the "wicked" child that either can be helped to be kinder and more tolerant to the other.

Students must also learn the importance of good administration as a means of providing for people the service they need when they need it and in the form that will help them best. There is also much that they must learn about the complexity of the social services and how these actually operate in practice. Students must also learn to co-operate with colleagues and with members of other professions. For instance, it is important that they should realize the particular professional functions and ways of looking at things of teachers, doctors, health visitors, magistrates and others with whom they may need to co-operate in the course of their work. This development of a defined minimum standard of competence in practice is so vital that supervisors' reports on students are given equal weight with theoretical studies in deciding whether the student should receive the qualifying award.

In giving this picture of recent developments in education for social work I do not want for a moment to paint too rosy a picture or give the impression that things are very much better than they are. We have a very long way to go yet in a variety of directions. I do think, however, that at last we are essentially on the right road, not because we have necessarily achieved high standards, but because in spite of many defects and failures we have now evolved the educational structure and the teaching method that should enable us steadily to improve the content of the courses, and therefore to produce better practitioners, which after all is the purpose of training. Perhaps the most important element in this is that instead of vaguely hoping that if people learned enough about the social sciences and the social services they would become good social workers, we have begun to see that relevant knowledge from each of these subjects must be carefully identified, set in a larger framework, with the different parts interrelated with each other and focused upon the theory and practice of social work. Secondly, we are clear at last that knowledge does not automatically get translated into practice and that to achieve this is perhaps an even more difficult process than acquiring the knowledge itself.

In other words, education for a profession as distinct from academic learning as such has the three aspects of knowledge, skill and attitudes. This will be clear if we look for a moment at the characteristics of any profession. These include a base of knowledge largely derived from the particular professions supporting sciences (for instance, chemistry, physiology and biology in medicine), followed by the translation of this knowledge into the practice methods charactertistic of that profession. As an example, we can think of the ways in which the teacher uses knowledge of the thought world of the child in evolving appropriate educational methods for teaching a class of small children. Thirdly, every responsible profession develops a code of ethics. Some elements in these codes, whether written or assumed, are the same for all the helping professions; for example, giving an impartial service to those who need it, irrespective of one's own likes and dislikes, or the person's status, ability to pay, class, creed or colour. The principle of confidentiality, of respecting people's personal affairs and professional confidence, is also taken for granted. There are various other elements in a professional code, but perhaps the most basic ethic of all, and the most difficult to express other than in rather general almost sentimental terms, is respect for human beings by virtue of their humanity; and the commitment to do everything possible that promotes their welfare and nothing that impedes it. In other and simpler terms, really wanting to help people for their own sake and not for personal gratification.

If we regard these three aspects, knowledge, skill and attitudes, as being in their different ways equally vital to professional practice, then it follows that we must work out ways of enabling students to absorb them during their professional education. I have indicated some of the means by which this is being done in social work education at present, though naturally we are only in the comparatively early stages of this development and have a very great deal still to learn. For one thing, we do not yet know at all precisely what constitutes good professional practice. We are also faced with tremendous problems in trying to cover the range of subject matter adequately and giving students sufficient time for fieldwork. In addition to this, it is unfortunate that in social work, as in teacher training, students undertake theoretical studies in one setting and their practical training in another. This naturally makes it more difficult to bring about close and effective relations between theory and practice.

I also think we need to devote very much more time and effort than we have done so far to a better understanding of skill learning and how to apply this in teaching social work practice. In a good deal of professional education, whether for social work or for other professions, we have perhaps been insufficiently aware of the three necessary stages in this, which are: first, the acquisition of knowledge, second its application and third the development of practice skills. Knowing something is by no means identical with being able to relate that knowledge appropriately to particular examples; and furthermore being able to perceive that x is an example of y is not at all the same thing as being able to do something effective about it. Any good professional education must therefore give students sufficient time and opportunities for whatever is the appropriate practice in regard to each of these three aspects of learning. Naturally, this also entails careful use of different educational methods and learning experiences for each of them. The challenge of what to teach, how to teach it and how to evaluate the results has become both urgent and stimulating, since at long last we have begun to see that the first essential question to ask is not "What shall we put into the course?" but "What are we training for?". As we have become more clear about these three elements in professional social work education it has also become apparent that courses must be lengthened. If students leave with merely a smattering of ill-digested knowledge or a fragile skill these will evaporate in the rough and tumble of practice. The minimum length of training thus tends nowadays to be 2 years, except for students who already have a university qualification in social studies.

All this time I have been doing the unpardonable thing of speaking about social casework as though it were the whole of social work, for it will be realized that practically all the developments I have described relate primarily to casework. For various reasons which it is hard to understand fully, training for group work, including the youth service, has lagged behind advances not only in the training of caseworkers, but also in their more effective use and support in employment. It is a long time now since I was connected with the Youth Service in those fruitful days during and immediately after the war when the Ministry of Education promoted training, and when developments in the university and other courses were a good deal more lively and hopeful than in casework. I do not know why this situation changed, why some of the best courses were discontinued and a sense of direction and advance was lost. It may be instructive to look more closely in this regard at the impetus to the developments which I described in casework. If this came partly through visiting teachers from American post-graduate schools of social work, why were we not able to profit from the group work teachers who also came here, ready to help us to take hold of and use what they had to give? The impetus in casework teaching has undoubtedly come also from two other sources, a government department—the Home Office—with its two training councils in child care and probation, together with the statutory Council for Training in Social Work; and from the strong and active professional associations, notably in medical and psychiatric social work. All of these have put punch, drive, financial resources and manpower into the improvement and expansion of training.

After the publication of the Albemarle Report,[2] the policy of the Department of Education and Science seems to have been to concentrate training for the Youth Service almost wholly at the National College for the Training of Youth Leaders, apart from the long-established course at Westhill and one or two others.* The Central Training Council in Child Care, and the Council for Training in Social Work have on the other hand pursued a policy of stimulating professional training courses in universities and colleges of further education all over the country. This has made it possible to raise the level of local practice by regular work with supervisors, and to reap the advantages of concurrent rather than block fieldwork placements. Experience has also shown that one-year courses are too short for people without prior experience or a sound base in social studies. Moreover, to concentrate on minimum basic training increases numbers quickly but does not produce the advanced practitioners, supervisors, consultants and group work teachers whom the service needs if it is to develop a real sense of purpose and direction. The Youth Service seems to have been living in a state of emergency ever since its birth in 1939, so far as training and a total strategy for a professional Service is concerned.

Of course, I know the controversies about whether youth leadership is primarily a branch of social work or of teaching. I also know the argument that social work is only concerned with the

*This course is to be discontinued (1970), and four two-year courses in youth and community work are to be started (E.Y.).

distressed, the deprived or the deviant and is therefore not relevant to work with normal young people. This is about as apposite as to say that teachers are concerned with normal children and therefore have nothing to offer to maladjusted or handicapped children. Or that doctors treat sickness and therefore have nothing to do with health. The essence of social work lies in helping people to achieve better and more satisfactory levels of social functioning, to overcome handicaps in themselves and their circumstances that impede this, and to become more effective (more of a person as the Americans would say), in their positive development. At one end of the scale this undoubtedly means long-term support to problem families, or short-term help to someone in the crisis of bereavement or desertion. But it also includes helping groups of people of different ages or in different circumstances to develop richer and more satisfying relations with other people, to discover how to do things for themselves and to develop the social skills that will enable them to become more independent, more competent, more on top of things. This to me is the essence of social work with groups or communities, and the programme, the premises, the activities and all the rest of it are means to this end not ends in themselves. But is this so very far removed from some of the aims of education too?

What about next steps? What are the likely or desirable developments in social work education that might bring the three methods, casework, group work and work with communities closer together? I can only indicate a few straws blowing in the wind, though there are certainly others too. Already it is ceasing to be accurate to talk about training for casework alone. For a long time, students taking these courses have been demanding teaching about group relations and some opportunity for practice. The result is that now a considerable number of courses are adding such teaching; at least one college has recently made a full-time appointment; and there is an eager search for groupwork records produced in this country. The development of fieldwork placements is starting in two ways. One is by providing seminars for practising groupworkers, in the Youth Service or elsewhere, so that they may begin to be able to supervise students. The other is through the use of group methods with clients in social agencies primarily geared to giving a casework service; for example group discussions with would-be adopters, with patients in a hospital ward, with prisoners' wives, with parents having difficulty with their children or children having difficulty with their parents, with acting out adolescents, with handicapped people or old people—and so on. In addition to all this, the Williams Committee on the training of residential staffs has recently produced a report, *Caring for People*,[3] in which it recommends a 2-year training with the primary emphasis on group relations in residential situations.

We have talked a good deal about community development since the mid-1940's but thought of it in terms of the developing countries. Now we have become conscious that the essential processes in working with local communities are the same here as in Africa or Asia. Moreover, these processes rest on an undertsanding of human behaviour in group and inter-group situations, and how to help local people to gain more confidence and effectiveness in managing their affairs and making use of community resources. Actually, there is a considerable amount of work with local communities being done in this country and a new interest in it, but almost no development of professional education on the general lines I discussed earlier. Several years ago, the Gulbenkian Foundation set up a Study Group on Training for Community Work. Its task was to look at the present situation and to try to chart a desirable course for future developments.[4] We laboured hard and long on that Study Group, often seeming to flounder because the whole situation is so diffuse and the boundaries very misty. It seems clear, however, that knowledge of human behaviour drawn from sociology and psychology is as essential here as in casework; while the skill in application also rests largely on the disciplined use of relationships with groups and individuals, as well as knowing what community resources exist and how to make the best use of them.

Here, then, are four strands in the development of training for social work: first, well-established training for casework with some understanding of groupwork and community work being added to it; secondly, increasing use of groupwork methods in training for the Youth Service; thirdly, new attitudes towards training for residential work; and lastly, a new concern about training for community work. Heaven forbid that we should develop a series of watertight specializations in all these fields, as we did in the past in casework. It may be, indeed, that training for the Youth Service as such is an outmoded concept, that what we need is people whose training has made them skilled and perceptive in working with groups and local communities, no matter what the age composition or main interests or needs of these may be.

We shall only arrive at wise answers to these and other questions if we put a great deal of energy, thought, controlled experimentation, wise planning, and adequate resources into finding the way through. In our expanding social services it is quite as important to develop professional skills in helping normal people to cope with problems of social relations, as it is to provide individual casework services for those in severe difficulties. Let us hope, then, that in the next ten years we may see rapid advances in training for social work with groups and communities.

REFERENCES

1. JOAN E. MATTHEWS, *Working With Youth Groups*. U.L.P., 1966, p. 44.
2. MINISTRY OF EDUCATION, *The Youth Service in England and Wales*, (Albemarle Report), H.M.S.O., 1960.
3. GERTRUDE WILLIAMS, *Caring for People*, Allen & Unwin, 1967.
4. THE GULBENKIAN FOUNDATION, *Community Work and Social Change*, Longmans, 1968.

CHAPTER 10

Teaching, Social Work and Interprofessional Training

Maurice Craft

It was particularly interesting to have the opportunity of contributing to a conference and to a volume concerned with issues in the forefront of contemporary thinking about the Youth Service in Britain; and concerned, in particular, with the relationship of Youth Service to neighbouring specialisms and the emerging concept of interprofessional training and development. It has always seemed to me that to train students for distinct—but nonetheless closely related professional roles—in isolation from each other is extremely wasteful. We can surely no longer afford (if indeed we ever could) our national tradition of devising local, rule-of-thumb remedies to meet emerging social needs, and of allowing them to become institutionalized without regard to the shape and the rationale of the overall pattern of provision.

In September 1964, the Sociology Department at Edge Hill College of Education began a 3-year main course entitled *Social Work*, (and in due course this was followed by the development of 4-year B.Ed. degree, one-term in-service, and day-release courses in the same field). Edge Hill is a teacher training college which trains only teachers and not social workers, so this development was a somewhat unusual one. The three-year main course was designed to produce a "teacher/social worker", i.e. a teacher with a particular viewpoint, a *welfare* viewpoint, and was obviously not undertaken lightly and without a good deal of background thinking about the relationship between education and social welfare. It is this background thinking to which I propose to give most attention in this paper, partly because it seems to me to be one of the most

121

nportant aspects of this teacher/social worker development. And partly because it takes us right into the area of interprofessional development, which was the theme of the 3-day conference.

I propose, then, to consider the subject-matter of this paper in four parts:

(a) first, I will suggest that the modern conception of education is concerned with individual development, with socialization, with the norms and values of the wider society—and not simply with the crudely limited aims of order and literacy. And my conclusions here will be that the techniques, the professional insights, and to some extent the aims of social work are relevant to the practice of teaching.

(b) I will suggest, secondly, that there is a developing range of specialist roles which together constitute what might be called the school's *welfare function*, and that these roles form a bridge between the theory and practice of education and social work.

(c) Thirdly, I will say a little about the teacher/social worker concept, again in the context of the relationship of education and social work;

(d) and lastly, a few words about interprofessional training itself.

EDUCATION TODAY

First, then, what is education about?

Traditionally, we expect teachers to convey the basic skills— reading and writing. We expect them to equip children with some knowledge of the physical environment (the scientific and geographical perspectives) and of the historical evolution of the nation. We ask them to foster sensitivities regarded as desirable in our culture— music, art, dance, and a variety of practical and aesthetic handcrafts. We also ask teachers to mould character, to exert an influence on the development of particular attitudes and values in children.

The way in which these areas of the child's basic socialization are fulfilled varies widely of course. A great many primary schools today offer a most impressive display of professional skills (old buildings and large classes apart). But in many secondary schools we may find a large number of *dysfunctional* elements. The "instrumental" (or instructional) aspect may be so arid, or so ill-adjusted to the life-experience and perception of children from the local environment as to be extremely inefficient. The amount of real learning which takes place may be quite negligible. The more "expressive" aspect—music, the arts, etc.—may be very limited in its interpretation. The use of the modern idiom may be considered taboo, for example. The "normative" aspect, the transmission of values, may involve a clash of social class-based ideas of what is or is not proper, that may succeed only in alienating the children from school. Where these dysfunctional elements exist, the ability of children may actually *deteriorate*,[1] and the school may actually *foster* delinquency.[2]

Now if this is what education *can* be like in some of our towns and cities, what *ought* it to be like? The modern conception of education would certainly accept the "instrumental" function of imparting knowledge and understanding; but it would seek to achieve it through exploration and discovery, so that the child makes his own steps and experiences the exhilaration of learning, rather than being presented with the facts and experiencing only the rather less exciting process of being taught. Like the social worker, the modern teacher is a *facilitator*, an organizer of learning experiences, rather than a source of ready-made solutions and pre-digested knowledge.[3] Like the social worker, the teacher must be sensitive to the limitations presented by social background. The home environment and social pressures experienced by children will vary between rural and urban areas, and sometimes also between different types of urban area–central city district, the slums of the transition zone, the various rings of suburban housing—and between new towns, expanded towns, satellite towns and industrial estates.[4]

In addition to the pressures of poor housing and overcrowding, ill-health, unemployment, large families, poverty, racial friction and so on, which exist in many areas, the teacher, like the social worker in relation to his client, needs an understanding of the child's capacity to *communicate*, to *receive communication*, and to *learn*, through the delicate mechanism of language. Professor Bernstein's distinction between the "restricted" and "elaborated" verbal codes of children at different social levels has given us an insight into this crucial area.[5] The insights of *social psychology* (which are equally relevant in social work), require the teacher to be aware of classroom and peer group pressures, to be aware of the significance of the child's self-concept (or self image), and so on.

These kinds of observation on our contemporary view of education apply of course, not only to the "instrumental" (instructional) elements in the teacher's work, but also to the more "expressive" functions (e.g. music, movement, painting, pottery). The modern view would be that these latter activities release tensions, or satisfy a desire to be creative or artistic. "Here there is no attempt to build up skills as the main purpose; each child is releasing energy from within himself, not absorbing information or practising techniques."[6] So today, in a great many schools there would be less emphasis on the teacher-dominated rehearsing of scales or steps, and more on the child's exploration of harmony or movement or colour, within a learning context devised by the teacher. Similarly, the "normative" environment in the more forward-looking schools has moved beyond concern for clean shoes or fingernails (important as these may be), to the cultivation of concern in children for individual rights in the context of obligations to the group.

The emphasis in modern education lies with the development of a wider and wider segment of each individual's unique range of endowments, within the limits imposed by the needs of other individuals. And I would suggest that this *creative* function is paralleled in social work where the caseworker seeks to mobilize the resources of his client.

The origins of these ideas lie outside education and social welfare; they lie in our evolving social and political philosophy which, in the mid-twentieth century, places infinite value on the worth of the individual human being, granting him rights to life, health, employment, education, religious and cultural freedom, and the right to choose who shall govern him. As western industrial societies have grown more complex, the proliferating need for industrial and commercial skills has given impetus to this emphasis on individual worth. It has emphasized the need to exploit all the reserves of ability we have, the need to combat loss of interest and deteriorating performance at school, early leaving, the "brain drain" —in the interests not only of the individuals concerned, but also of society as a whole.*

To summarize, then, the contemporary view of education places emphasis on learning rather than teaching; on growth and development; on individual curiosity and the satisfaction of personal achievement, often through the medium of the small group. The modern teacher is a *facilitator* of this learning process, as is the social worker in the casework or groupwork process. To "facilitate" requires knowledge of human growth and behaviour, small group relations, and such aspects of the social fabric as the social class structure, family patterns and value systems, and urban processes. Again, these are common areas of basic professional study for both teachers and social workers (and here I include youth leaders and youth employment officers).

I am *not* saying that teachers and social workers are interchangeable. Each specialism is distinctive. But while the *ameliorative* role of the social worker (the problem element) is perhaps relatively less important in teaching, the *creative* role overlaps much more extensively. As Davies and Gibson have written in their book on Youth Service, *The Social Education of the Adolescent*, . . . "to help individuals from maladjustment to greater adjustment (as is customarily attempted in social work) is not essentially at variance (either in principle or purpose) with helping individuals from normal adjustment to greater self-expression and fulfilment . . . ."[7]

THE SCHOOL'S WELFARE FUNCTION

The second area which we might consider, in relation to our theme, is the school's *welfare function*, for here, too, I think we have a bridge between education and social work.

*Discussed in H. LYTTON and M. CRAFT (Eds.), *Guidance on Counselling in British Schools*, Arnold, 1969.

The training of "school counsellors" has just begun in this country and diploma courses are now in existence at four universities (Exeter, Keele, Reading and Swansea). Their aims vary a little, but by and large they are designed to train a specialist in educational, vocational and personal guidance who will also have contacts with neighbourhood welfare services (child guidance, probation, children's department), and with parents. This is a most significant development for it recognizes that the school has a vital responsibility in a largely "non-pedagogic" field.

Up till now, the school's *welfare* role has been represented by the school medical, dental, and psychological services; secondly, by the education welfare officer (or the school care committee) who has maintained a link with families in difficulty whose children are irregular in attendance or inadequately clothed; and thirdly, by the provision of school meals and milk. But the training of school counsellors seems to imply that the traditional system of requiring *all* teachers to maintain a "pastoral" oversight of their pupils is none too satisfactory; and that even where the appointments of housemaster or careers teacher exist there is need for some special training.

I personally welcome this development, but I rather doubt if any one counsellor will be able to fulfil what seem to me to be four closely related functions:

educational guidance which aims to discover the child's abilities and disabilities, and to ensure an appropriate choice of course and appropriate remedial measures if needed;

vocational guidance, which dove-tails into this process of careful assessment by a variety of means, over the *whole* of a child's school career. In the final year or two, vocational guidance adds an introduction to the world of work through special teaching schemes, visits and work experience, etc., and close co-operation with the youth employment officer as placement and follow-up specialist;

personal guidance, which can hardly be divorced from the other two, but involves mainly those children who show evidence of stress and disturbance: the persistently truanting child, the overly aggressive, or silent and withdrawn child, the delinquent, etc.,[8] and fourth,

contact with neighbourhood welfare services and with parents: referral of problems to local social work agencies, and participation in area co-ordinating committees may be possible, but home visiting is tremendously time consuming and can hardly be feasible in addition to the other three functions.

I suspect that few local education authorities will find it possible to appoint non-teaching school counsellors in any numbers for some years to come, and the supply, in any case, will remain very small indeed. So for these and other reasons, I would favour the greater use of part-teaching (in-service trained) specialists who would divide up some of the separate functions I have mentioned, and I would envisage the school counsellor being used as a welfare *co-ordinator* within the large school or over a group of schools. The school "welfare team" would then include in-service trained careers staff (responsible, together with youth employment officers, for vocational guidance), and teacher/social workers (responsible for home-school links), amongst other specialist personnel.

Now this brief sketch of the school's *welfare function* perhaps indicates whole areas of common ground for teachers and social workers. At training level alone, there can surely be little doubt that common, generic training for school counsellors, school social workers (at present employed by the Glasgow Education Department, and trained at Reading University), and youth employment officers should be possible.

THE TEACHER/SOCIAL WORKER

The teacher/social worker, the third point I wished to say a little about, would ideally be a member of a school welfare team, responsible for liaison with parents, with the education welfare officer, and with local social workers. In practice, the teacher social/worker will probably be a part-teaching welfare specialist with some responsibilities for personal guidance, referral and follow-up, parent–teacher contact, and the maintenance of an adequate record system—a very sizeable set of responsibilities (and very nearly a one-man team, in fact).

The essence of the teacher/social worker idea is *prevention*. We really cannot go on saying that behaviour problems or study difficulties would have been smaller and less intractable had we only spotted them in time. We need to do something about spotting them in time.

Ideally, again, this aspect of teacher education might be strengthened for *all* teachers. But with the continuing development of experimental school curricula, teaching methods, "educational technology" (i.e. teaching machines, C.C.T.V., etc.), the impact of secondary school reorganization, and of the B.Ed. degree, competition for additional time (or a bid for the restructuring of the College core studies in education) are hardly feasible. It seems much more realistic to offer specialized training in early detection, in accurate referral to local social workers, and in parent–teacher contact to a *few* students through a main course, and this is the pattern at Edge Hill where about forty students each year now study social work.*

The teacher/social worker appointments so far created by L.E.A.s (e.g., Accrington, Blackpool, Portsmouth) are part-teaching appointments, and as this is likely to be the future pattern, the Edge Hill course was designed to equip teacher/social workers for remedial teaching, work with immigrant children, and other special skills, in addition to their basic studies in psychology, sociology, social policy and social administration. An extremely important part of the course is the section on the "principles and practice of social work", which included theoretical work taught by practising social workers (there is one full-time social worker on the staff of the Department of Sociology and several part-time), and which also included a very wide range of visits and attachments to social work agencies over the 3 years.

But there are two very important things to say about this "extended teaching role". First, the teacher/social worker as trained at

*Written in July 1968 (Eds.).

Edge Hill College is basically a teacher not a social worker, and each student must achieve the normal level of professional competence in teaching. Although a number might be aspiring social workers who decided to come into teaching in order to take up this kind of work; and although all tend to have much in common with social workers in terms of professional outlook at the end of the course, they are *not* equipped to undertake casework, and family therapy would be the responsibility of local social work agencies (i.e. they would *refer* problem cases).

Second, the teacher/social worker's role is not completely devoted to the preventive and therapeutic measures I have described. He or she would have a major responsibility in making contact with those parents whose life experience has led them to place little importance on education; or whose interest in education is frustrated by sheer lack of information about courses, careers and so on. At this *informational* level, the teacher/social worker would have a great deal to do (perhaps through a parent–teacher association which organizes regular meetings), in telling parents about the curriculum of the school, in explaining modern teaching methods, in discussing career opportunities. Many P.T.A.s, of course, go beyond this into the realm of "parent education", where all manner of problems related to child-upbringing are considered.

But for those parents who do not attend this type of formal gathering as a matter of social tradition, or who usually return late from a day of manual work, the only possibility of arousing or of developing an interest in the work of the school and the only hope, perhaps, of getting them to encourage a clever son or daughter to stay on after fifteen years may be a *personal visit*, and this would be a major responsibility of the teacher/social worker. It would not be a visit concerned with "trouble"—problems connected with behaviour or work, the problems of the deviant child—but one concerned with the extremely important task of drawing the parents of quite normal children into the work of the school, in the interests of those children.

A great deal of post-war research in Britain and the United States has related poor school achievement and early leaving to a low level of "parental interest", and so, although home-visiting might, for some teacher/social workers (and for some parents) raise problems of role conflict, it seems that this is a mechanism well worth trying. A number of researches have measured parental interest at a very crude level, for example as expressed by the preferred school-leaving age, the type of secondary education sought for the child, or the provision of homework facilities. Others have involved more subtlety and have considered the pattern of child-rearing practices, the development of "achievement motivation" through the interaction of specific kinds of parental behaviour, or the job satisfaction of parents.[9]

The Plowden Committee attempted to gauge parental interest in education through numbers of visits made to the school and attendance at school functions. But we are still a long way from the accurate measurement of basic values which lie far more deeply and which are reflected in differing attitudes to education at different social levels. For example, do all social classes have the same concern with planning, and with individualism, or with taking an active rather than a passive role in life? Is there the same concern with education for girls as for boys in different social groups (including immigrant groups)? What are the levels of occupational aspiration in different subcultures? (And it is important to remember that there are at least two and perhaps four identifiable subcultures within the working class, to say nothing of regional variations.)[10]

All this is by way of theoretical justification for the notion of a teacher/social worker.[11] It is a specialized role which, I suggest, indicates some of the areas of study and of work which teachers and social workers have in common. I have already referred to other points of contact—the teacher as a facilitator, the sensitivity to interpersonal relations, the importance of social background in educational planning, the school's welfare function.

INTERPROFESSIONAL TRAINING

Another way of studying the relations between education and social work might be to examine such social work basic principles as *acceptance* or *self determination*, or *confidentiality*,[12] and this brings me to the last topic I should like to consider, interprofessional training.

Acceptance is perceiving and dealing with a client as he really is, with all "his strengths and weaknesses, his congenial and uncongenial qualities, his positive and negative feelings, his constructive and destructive attitudes and behaviour, maintaining all the while a sense of the client's innate dignity and personal worth".[13] Is this not the attitude of the good teacher to whom the individual child is of supreme worth, regardless of social class, religion or racial origins?[14]

Self determination involves the social caseworker in stimulating the client's potential for self-direction, and helping him to recognize and exploit the appropriate resources of his own personality and of the community, subject only to the client's capacity for such decision-making and to the limits of the law. I have already suggested that modern educational theory places the onus of discovery on the child, and that the teacher acts as a facilitator in the learning process, subject, or course, to the age and ability of the child and to his capacity for self-direction.

Confidentiality is the preservation of private and personal information concerning the client which is disclosed in the professional casework relationship, and I would suggest that this is as applicable in teaching as it is in social work.

Finally, social workers talk of *controlled emotional involvement* as the technique for directing the therapeutic relationship purposefully and at the same time responding sensitively and appropriately to the client's feelings. I would suggest that this has its counterpart in teaching, where involvement *automatically* accompanies the relationships between teacher and taught which are central to the learning process. The primary school teacher in particular may find it difficult to avoid a high degree of emotional involvement, as Professor Blyth has argued. His (or her) role cannot ". . . be discharged with even that degree of detachment which a doctor or a trained social worker is expected to display";[15] and this perhaps emphasizes the need for self-awareness, a sensitivity cultivated in social work.

Derek Jehu in his book *Learning Theory and Social Work*[16] provides us with a second and most interesting illustration of the common ground between education and social work. He describes how, for example, conditioning, learning by imitation, or insight learning can help provide an explanation of human behaviour and can be used in social work treatment. These are traditionally fundamental areas of study for professional teaching, and Jehu provides a fascinating and well-documented account of how, similarly, they can be considered central to the work of the professional caseworker. One might, of course, argue that the insights into how people learn which are provided by learning theory must be supplemented by the insights into social norms and expectations which are provided by social psychology and sociology in the study of small groups, sub-cultures, and social institutions.* But then these too are central areas of study which are common to both teaching and social work.

I think it is important that we pay attention to such common areas of study, and that we seriously consider the advantages of joint training if we are right in judging the functional overlaps in education and social work to greatly outweigh the functional differences. Professor Ben Morris, for example, in discussing and defining the contribution of psychology to education, claims its relevance as a foundation study for social workers (and perhaps also for doctors) as well as for teachers.[17]

A third example of recent interprofessional thinking is provided by Peter Nokes in his book *The Professional Task in Welfare Practice*. Nokes argues that teachers (including those in remedial and special education) and those social workers who are based in institutions (for example in borstals or mental hospitals) share a *diffuse* professional role. They do not possess any clearly definable skills, any distinctive technology (compared, say, with surgery or medicine), which " . . . to the onlooker [would] appear markedly different from . . . ordinary social intercourse".[18] Neither teachers nor social workers, on the whole, can place precise outlines on

* And which are perhaps just as important as psycho-dynamic theories of the subconscious drives that influence behaviour. See P. Leonard, *Sociology in Social Work*, Routledge and Kegan Paul, 1966.

either their aims or their professional achievement—except, of course, for those of them who take a very limited, instrumental view of their role (getting children through examinations, say; or handing out cash benefits).[19]

None of the foregoing discussion must be taken as meaning that education and social work are the same thing; they are distinctive and separate professional roles. But it would seem to me that there is sufficient overlap of perspective and of basic principles to justify interprofessional training at certain levels.

Let us take a further example of the relationship between education and social work. On the margins of education are a number of specialized teaching roles which shade off into social work. I have already mentioned the school counsellor, the teacher/social worker, the careers teacher; and one might also include remedial specialists, or teachers of immigrant children. Or at a different level, teachers in special education (i.e. for mentally or physically handicapped children), or teachers in approved schools. As Gordon Rose writes, "There is . . . an area in teaching that is, in a wide sense, social training, and overlaps a good deal with what we tend to think of as social work", and he goes on to argue persuasively for special social work (group work) training for approved school staff.[20] Like other writers, Rose elsewhere suggests that teaching in primary and secondary schools in difficult areas also shares much with the aims and techniques of social work.[21]

Youth leadership is one of the most interesting of these "marginal" roles, for it has roots in both education and social work. To the extent that it is concerned with the development of potentialities it is related to education. To the extent that it uses the basic techniques of social group work it is part of social work.[22] But then, for me, the principles and practice of social work are to quite a large extent applicable in education; and the development of potentialities is a recognized aim of social work. So the current discussion (reflected, for example, by Raymond Woolfe)[23] of where youth leadership belongs is a somewhat sterile one I think, and it seems far more constructive to look ahead to a rationalization of training, to *inter-professional* training, where teachers, youth leaders, educational welfare officers (or school social workers), school counsellors, youth employment officers and other caseworkers and groupworkers are trained side by side, and not in separate institutions, isolated from fellow professionals.

The development of interprofessional training (as Professor Tibble writes in chapter 11 of this book) has long been a topic of discussion, and was raised again by the Plowden Committee in their report in 1967. A disadvantage of the present pattern of teacher training they felt was that colleges of education train teachers only, that "a choice of career is forced on students at eighteen or earlier, before some know their own minds, and future teachers are segregated from those preparing for other types of work."[24] The Committee went on to recommend that there should be further experiment in the joint training of teachers and social workers (paras. 253 and 960) as had both the Robbins Report[25] (in para. 313) and the Newsom Report[26] (in paras. 293–4), in 1963, the latter specifically including youth leadership and the youth employment service in its recommendations for joint training.

These are the most recent references to interprofessional development in government reports but they are by no means the only ones to have appeared. In 1965, the report on *The Future Development of the Youth Employment Service*[27] (paras. 194–6) stated that while youth employment is a specialized field requiring specialized courses of training, nonetheless there might well be gains in joint training in common core studies for youth employment officers, teachers, youth leaders, social caseworkers, and personnel managers. Such joint training, the committee felt, would widen the horizons of youth employment officers, facilitate more fruitful relations with other professional colleagues in the field, and would perhaps aid transfer from youth employment to a related field later on if an officer so desired. Basic training apart, the committee felt that interprofessional in-service courses and conferences are increasingly valuable.

Earlier, in 1960, the Albemarle Report on the Youth Service[28] had in fact taken a step away from interprofessionalism by recommending the establishment of a national college for the training of youth leaders. But this was felt to be an emergency measure and the college was given a limited life* (paras. 266–8). Furthermore, the committee clearly underlined their belief that recruitment to youth leadership would continue to come mainly from teaching, social work, and "mature persons with a natural gift for leadership"; that youth leadership should become a more recognized avenue of training in the colleges of education (which it now has); that the area training organizations for teaching should supervise all recognized courses of training for youth leadership; and that transfer to "other professional work in education or the social services" (para. 247) should be made easier (pp. 72–9).

The Underwood Committee's report on maladjusted children in 1955[29] argued for a generic training in social work and for easier transfer within the field of social work (pp. 117–18); but it also recommended interprofessional training in para. 405 where the joint training of educational psychologists, psychiatrists, and psychiatric social workers is proposed as a good basis for successful team work later on, and where it is suggested that if the joint training is based in a university department of psychology or education there might be additional gains in perspective.

Going farther back, to 1944, the McNair Report on the supply, recruitment and training of teachers and youth leaders[30] recommended a 3-year course of training for each role and easier transfer from one to the other (pp. 104–5). The Committee also felt that initiatives in interprofessional training in colleges of education might be encouraged (para. 249), although they appeared to prefer "parallel" rather than "joint" interprofessional training (i.e. teachers and youth leaders training side by side in the same institution

* Some current opinions favour an *advanced* training role for the National College. Initial training might then be undertaken elsewhere "within more generic courses" and might equip students with a more widely applicable qualification. (See "Doomed service?" in *New Society*, 20 July 1967, pp. 90–1.) A more recent comment proposes an *interprofessional* role for the National College. Its numbers should be expanded, it is said, and it should embrace " . . . some of the interdisciplinary hinterland between education and social work—community development, educational welfare and lay leadership." (B. Davis, "Leader trouble", in *New Society*, 16 May 1968, p. 716).

under the "area training authority" for teacher training, rather than combining all or part of their respective courses (paras. 366 and 370). But the committee was emphatic that the *segregation* of teachers and of youth leaders in training is most undesirable. Two years earlier in 1942, Professor G. D. H. Cole had published his celebrated condemnation of segregation in training in a most relevant essay:[31]

> It seems to me highly undesirable on social grounds to isolate those who are to become teachers, during their training, in a specialized institution consisting wholly of teachers in training, instructed wholly by persons wholly engaged in training teachers, and cooped up residentially in a sort of a teachers' monkey house apart from ordinary human beings who propose to follow other occupations.*

This is quoted, almost a quarter of a century later, in 1966, in the P.E.P. report *Problems Facing the Teaching Profession*, which points out that the increased *size* of interprofessional institutions facilitates a more extensive range of courses and of staff resources, apart from the possible broadening of perspectives in the student body (p. 226). But it remains a fact that most teachers pass directly from school to training college and back to school with no further broadening experience other than vacation work or holiday travel. (Although it is conceded that many colleges now offer an extremely varied and stimulating three or four year course.) Perhaps the development of teacher training in technical colleges will make a contribution here. †

So we may perhaps summarize, with David Ayerst, that "Learning to be a teacher is no longer the sheltered life it was, though it is

* The majority of teachers, writes Professor Robin Pedley, "have never experienced . . . (through university education) . . . the rich variety of contacts with able minds geared to widely different interests. Their world has been the comparatively narrow world of the training college—*a world of teachers and would-be teachers only . . .* " (my italics). *The Comprehensive School*, Penguin, 1963, p. 195.

† The Younghusband Report (1959) seems to have envisaged an interprofessional element in further education, (para. 889) *Report of the Working Party on Social Workers*, H.M.S.O., 1959. So far as the proposed *Polytechnics* are concerned, there are suggestions that they might incorporate colleges of education, (A.T.C.D.E. *Newssheet*, April 1968, p. 12), and this seems to be planned in Leeds. ("Polytechnic muddle", in *New Society*, 29 February 1968, p. 310).

still true, and perhaps unfortunate, that you train only with those who are going to teach and that the certificate you get at the end is not valuable . . . to serve as a qualification for a wide range of occupations."[32]

CONCLUSION

Lest my argument is misunderstood, may I stress this, that there seems to be little doubt that the proliferation of roles is a legitimate response to the proliferation of distinctive needs in an advanced industrial society. But the proliferation of *avenues of training* is far less fully justified.

I would be the first to argue that specialization of roles *within* teaching for example, is proceeding apace; but I would still feel that the basic professional training for infant, junior or secondary school teachers (or for staff in say technical schools, special schools or approved schools) should be largely common to all. And much the same is true of the specializations *within* social work,[33] and of the relationship of *teaching and social work*. In his essay on "The School and Mental Health",[34] Professor Bantock claims that teaching should not be confused with therapy, and one would certainly support this view. But as I said at the beginning, it seems extremely wasteful to duplicate training when teachers, caseworkers and group workers all undergo exposure to very similar basic areas of study. A common generic training followed by specialization would seem far more rational, and as the Plowden Report stated, "should encourage closer collaboration in the field" (para. 960).*

* Closer collaboration in the field seems a very obvious and desirable benefit which might follow from interprofessional training. The Hunt Report, *Immigrants and the Youth Service*, H.M.S.O., 1967, stressed the value of close contact between youth workers and social workers, not merely to aid effective referral but also to improve the general quality of service offered by both (para. 263). Similarly, the recent Home Office paper, *Children in Trouble* (Cmnd. 3601), H.M.S.O., 1968, envisages close collaboration and co-operation between magistrates, police, social workers and teachers in the prevention and treatment of juvenile delinquency. At periodic local meetings to review the working of the proposed new procedures, "Teachers . . . will take part . . . and children's

The situation at Westhill College of Education where teachers, youth leaders and community centre wardens train together; or at Moray House College of Education in Edinburgh where teachers, youth and community workers and social caseworkers train together, are examples of what might be done. As so many governmental committees have pointed out, *easier transfer* from professional work in one area of education and the social services to another could be a most valuable by-product of interprofessional training, and this might lend a new flexibility and efficiency to our very complex structure of social welfare provision. Indeed, the *overlapping recruitment* which already exists is both a rudimentary example of the benefits of this transfer of role, and also a further argument in favour of interprofessional development.

Most youth leaders and many youth employment officers for example, will continue to be drawn from teaching and the social services.[35] The Crowther Committee proposed that county college staff should be drawn from youth leaders or social workers (para. 298)[36] and this may to some extent be true in further education today. The Underwood Committee estimated that educational psychologists would continue to be recruited largely from the teaching profession* (pp. 105 and 111) and noted that teachers are among those also trained as psychiatric social workers (para. 433).[37]

The picture is a fascinating if complicated one. Let us hope that as the demand for teachers and social workers increasingly outpaces the supply, we shall evolve more rational and productive patterns of training to meet the needs of our society.

Footnote from p. 137 (contd.)

departments will maintain close liaison with schools when considering the action to be taken in individual cases" (para. 18). Again the much earlier Ince Report (1945) recognized "that teachers, youth leaders and industrial and social welfare workers will all in practice have many contacts with the . . . [youth employment] . . . service and . . . [felt] . . . that their courses of training might therefore with advantage include material which will enable them to appreciate the work of vocational guidance". (*Report of the Committee on the Juvenile Employment Service*, H.M.S.O., 1945, para. 202.)

* As is often compulsorily the case in Europe. (See M. Reuchlin, *Pupil Guidance*, Council for Cultural Co-operation, 1964, p. 121.)

REFERENCES

1. See, for example, R. R. DALE and S. GRIFFITH, *Down Stream*, Routledge and Kegan Paul, 1965,

2. D. HARGREAVES in *Social Relations in a Secondary School*, Routledge and Kegan Paul, 1967, considers this process from the point of view of streaming.

3. PETER DAWS clearly describes this process in relation to the school counsellor in "What will the school counsellor do?" *Educational Research*, February 1967 (pp. 85–6).

4. Considered in S. J. EGGLESTON, *The Social Context of the School*, Routledge and Kegan Paul, 1967, (chap. 2), and in greater detail in W. A. L. BLYTH, *English Primary Education*, Routledge and Kegan Paul, 1965 (vol. 2, chap. 4).

5. D. LAWTON, *Social Class, Language and Education*, Routledge and Kegan Paul, 1968.

6. M. D. SHIPMAN, *The Sociology of the School*, Longmans Green, 1968.

7. B. D. DAVIES and A. GIBSON, *The Social Education of the Adolescent*, U.L.P., 1967 (chap. 9).

8. PETER DAWS, *op. cit.*

9. M. CRAFT (Ed.), *Family, Class and Education*, Longmans Green, 1970.

10. G. ROSE, *The Working Class*, Longmans Green, 1968.

11. See also M. CRAFT, J. RAYNOR and L. COHEN (Eds.), *Linking Home and School*, Longmans Green, 1967.

12. Discussed in F. H. PEDLEY, *Education and Social Work*, Pergamon, 1967 (chap. 1).

13. F. P. BIESTEK, *The Casework Relationship*, Allen & Unwin, 1965 (p. 72).

14. But there are some important qualifications in the teacher's acceptance, because of the nature of his socializing role. See M. Craft, "The identity of the teacher: a commentary", in W. TAYLOR (Ed.), *Towards a Policy for the Education of Teachers* (Proceedings of the Colston Research Society 1968), Butterworth Press, 1969.

15. W. A. L. BLYTH, *English Primary Education*, Routledge and Kegan Paul, 1967 (vol. 1, p. 173).

16. D. JEHU, *Learning Theory and Social Work*, Routledge and Kegan Paul, 1967.

17. B. MORRIS, "The contribution of psychology to the study of education," in J. W. TIBBLE (Ed.), *The Study of Education*, Routledge and Kegan Paul, 1966 (p. 157).

18. P. NOKES, *The Professional Task in Welfare Practice*, Routledge and Kegan Paul, 1967 (p. vii).

19. For a discussion of the notion of the diffuse professional roles of teachers and social workers as a *continuum*, see M. CRAFT in W. TAYLOR (Ed.), *op. cit.*

20. G. ROSE, *Schools for Young Offenders*, Tavistock, 1967 (chap. 8).

21. *Ibid.* See also J. PARTRIDGE, *Life in a Secondary Modern School*, Pelican, 1968 (pp. 177 *et seq.*), and also R. S. PETERS, *Ethics and Education*, Allen & Unwin, 1966 (pp. 82 *et seq.*).

22. J. E. MATTHEWS, *Working with Youth Groups*, U.L.P., 1966 (pp. 46–8).

23. R. WOOLFE, The future of the Youth Service, in *Youth Service*, December 1966. See also the subsequent correspondence in *Youth Service*, April and May 1967.

24. Central Advisory Council for Education (England), *Children and Their Primary Schools*, H.M.S.O., 1967 (para. 958).

25. *Higher Education*, H.M.S.O., 1963.

26. Central Advisory Council for Education (England), *Half Our Future*, H.M.S.O., 1963.

27. *The Future Development of the Youth Employment Service*, H.M.S.O., 1965.

28. *The Youth Service in England and Wales*, H.M.S.O., 1960.

29. *Report of the Committee on Maladjusted Children*, H.M.S.O., 1955.

30. *Teachers and Youth Leaders*, H.M.S.O., 1944.

31. G. D. H. COLE, "The aims of education" (1942), in *Essays in Social Theory*, Oldbourne, 1962.

32. D. AYERST, *Understanding Schools*, Penguin, 1967 (p. 68).

33. "Social workers are increasingly taking the view—and this is being reflected in training arrangements—that social work is *a single profession within which specialities should be subordinate to the profession as a whole*, in much the same way as medical specialities are subordinate to the profession of medicine" (my italics). *Social Work and the Community*, (Cmnd. 3065), H.M.S.O., 1966 (para. 44).

34. G. H. BANTOCK, "The school and mental health", in *Education, Culture and the Emotions*, Faber, 1967 (pp. 23–43).

35. See *The Youth Service in England and Wales*, *op. cit.* (para. 248); and also *The Future Development of the Youth Employment Service*, *op. cit.* (para. 159).

36. Central Advisory Council for Education (England), *15 to 18*, H.M.S.O., 1959.

37. *Report of the Committee on Maladjusted Children*, *op. cit.*

CHAPTER 11

Interprofessional Education

J. W. TIBBLE

IN THE late 1950's the initiative and enthusiasm of Dr. Paul Halmos brought together a group of people to explore the common problems met by those concerned with the training of social workers and of teachers. To enlist wider interest, a series of weekend conferences was organized at Keele, Leicester and Nottingham. These conferences were mainly concerned with curricular problems, in particular the contributions of psychology, sociology and philosophy to courses for social workers and teachers, the content of theory courses, and methods of teaching and learning. The talks given at these conferences and a summary of the discussions were published by Keele in a series of monographs.[1] Another outcome of the conferences was the setting up of a committee to consider ways of developing further and possibly implementing in practice some of the many ideas which the conferences had thrown up.

The committee decided that for some time at any rate the best plan would be not to hold further large conferences, now that the main ground had been covered, but to organize smaller working parties, of thirty to forty people to consider specific topics and push the thinking on these further. As was to be expected, the large conferences, while indicating areas of common ground and concern, had also emphasized the many differences which existed among the members of the different professions. Suggestions of possible common courses of training brought into action the defences which all professions build around their own particular set of professional

141

attitudes, techniques and practices. In this connection, the differences between teacher education and the education of social workers in general were much in evidence. The former had developed, in the course of the 130 years of its history, a common pattern of training, or rather two common patterns, the concurrent academic and professional courses of the Colleges of Education and the consecutive courses of degree work followed by a professional year in the University Departments or Colleges catering for graduates. In the social work field, a much greater diversity existed, both in terms of specialized needs and of administrative controls. It was also clear that some branches of social work, e.g. youth leaders, youth employment officers and educational psychologists, had closer contacts and affinities with the work of the schools than other branches.

The first working party, which met in Leicester in 1962, was mainly concerned with the exploration of these differences and with the search for common ground in terms of objectives, content of courses and techniques of training which would justify the planning of interprofessional education. Everyone agreed, and this was later endorsed by the Robbins Report, that professional isolation was undesirable and that there would be much gain from the informal and social contacts of students preparing for the various helping professions in the same institution. Should the communion go beyond this and involve at any rate some working together in common lecture courses and seminars? Could one go further still and envisage a course which prepared people generally for a number of helping professions including teaching, the choice not being made until the end of the course? At the first session, Professor Halmos had indeed outlined the case for an interprofessional tripos.

> The need for social learning and for training in "social skills" was shared in fact by a very wide range of professional people not only by teachers and social workers but also by administrators, and by managers in commerce and industry. The concept of generic training was essential here. Through it the desired end would be achieved.

The discussion which followed raised in one form or another the major issues which the working party was to return to again and again during the following day and a half of its deliberations. These were the need to be aware of the differences in role and function which exist between different members of the "helping professions". This particular issue tended to crystallize about the roles of the teacher and the social worker. Other issues related to the function of subjects, especially psychology and sociology, the function of field and practical work, especially in relation to group-centred learning situations; the commitment of the individual student to a particular profession; and the nature of an interprofessional curriculum.

One session, led by Professor W. A. C. Stewart explored the differences in role and function of teachers and social workers. It was asserted that teachers were best thought of as "enablers": they enabled learning to take place. Social workers were more concerned with *unlearning* and with *re-learning*, with socio-technical skills which had broken down or proved inadequate. It was also suggested that the relationship between teacher and child was mediated by the task they were engaged in, the learning of skills and knowledge embodied in the school curriculum. The relationship of social worker and client was a more direct one. Later, Professor F. Musgrove pointed out that the teacher's role was diffuse. Other professionals had a clearer picture of their roles and experienced a greater degree of emotional neutrality in it. There was also much ambiguity in the teacher's role. Teachers never knew when their job was finished and assessing results, except in the case of short-term examination results, was very difficult.

There is no doubt that this exploration of differences, including the professional defences present in the working party members, helped with the delineation of the common ground. The agreement reached on this was in the end quite surprising, in view of the "bristling" which had been evident earlier on. Then we found the social workers agreeing that subjects such as history, literature and language pursued "for their own sake" as in the teacher-training course, would be of value also in social work courses, since the inculcation of attitudes was as important as the acquiring of specific skills and knowledge. And both sides agreed that the "professional" studies, psychology, sociology and philosophy, were equally valuable in the same sense, as ingredients in the students' personal and cultural development. Thus, one could begin to question the somewhat arbitrary divisions of the traditional curricula, both for teachers and social workers, and a move in this direction would enable more common ground to be established both in terms of curricular content and in terms of attitudes and goals. One further common area that was touched on and explored more fully by subsequent working parties was the need to give practical training and fieldwork experience in all the courses under consideration, and the consequent need to consider the relationship between theory and practice.

The last session of the 1962 meeting of the working party, led by Professor A. J. Allaway, was devoted to setting out the various possibilities for interprofessional courses which had emerged in the course of the discussion. These were as follows: (1) an interprofessional tripos—envisaged as an initial course for those going on later into administrative work in the field of the helping professions; (2) a general degree course in a university or college; (3) an interprofessional diploma course (part-time); (4) the joint post-graduate training of teachers and social workers; (5) a residential full-time diploma in interprofessional studies at the post-graduate level; (6) discussion groups composed of qualified graduate teachers and social workers organized by extramural departments, institutes of education or departments of social studies; (7) joint Younghusband and college of education courses; (8) an interprofessional college; (9) the development of interprofessional courses in new universities; (10) meetings and conferences organized regionally and nationally on an interprofessional basis. Here, then, was a blueprint for future development.

The next working party, meeting at Bede College, Durham, 2 years later in 1964, took up two of the topics raised at Leicester for intensive consideration. The first Leicester working party had been mainly a ground-clearing, or mind-clearing operation. At Durham seeds were sown; several later developments affecting teacher education had their origins in the Bede discussions. The first of these was a further consideration of the nature of the theoretical studies in interprofessional courses. This in the first place was very much an argument between those on the one hand who stressed the need for academic rigour, in, say, the sociology of education courses, that would make them not inferior in this subject to the sociology courses in a university arts or social science degree course; and on the other hand, those who stressed the vocational value of the subject and perhaps were reluctant to see education broken up into specialized aspects at all. But through the frank discussion of this issue, there began to appear ways of avoiding this opposition, of seeing how the sociology or psychology studied in the interprofessional courses could be specifically relevant to the needs of the profession in question without being less rigorous and challenging, indeed becoming more so by achieving maximum student involvement.[2] The more recent development of B.Ed. courses in colleges of education has made even more urgent the need to find a solution to this problem. Otherwise, there is a risk of creating in the colleges of education the counterpart of the class distinction between academic and practical which has so bedevilled the development of secondary education in the last fifty years.

The second topic which the Durham working party investigated was the place of practical work in the various interprofessional courses, in particular the role and function of the supervisor in this field and the relation between the supervision provided by the college or department and that provided by the school or agency. A demonstration of a simulated social work supervision session at Durham made it clear that teacher education might gain much from looking over the professional fence, and indeed this was the starting point for applications which will be referred to later in this account. Certainly, the Durham working party demonstrated the seminal value of the interprofessional approach: in the comparative setting, practices sanctified by time and tradition could more readily be questioned and reconsidered.

The third working party was held at the college of education in Leicester in 1966 and marked a further stage in the development of the interprofessional movement. Its purpose was twofold: first, to find out what was being attempted in the way of interprofessional courses, by collecting together those already active in promoting or taking part in such schemes; and second, to clarify the function and purpose of the national committee set up by the last Keele Conference.

Reports from members showed that quite a number of the proposals made in 1962 had by now been put into practice. Thus, Mr. Maurice Craft gave an account of the main course in Social Work taken by a group of teacher trainees at Edge Hill College of Education. Mr. C. J. Gill described the new course for education counsellors at the University of Keele. Mr. John Simmonds described the joint course of initial training for social workers and graduate teachers at Sussex University. Reference was also made to full- and part-time courses for workers in residential institutions—approved schools and children's homes—who need the skills both of teachers and of social workers; and to advanced courses run by institutes of education (e.g. courses in child development, or in the psychology and sociology of education) which are open to both teachers and social workers. There was also a session in which Miss Irene Caspari and Mr. John Eggleston described the experiments they had undertaken at Leicester University in applying a social-work type of supervision to the school practice situation in teacher training.

It is the common practice in the colleges of education for lecturers to supervise students by paying visits once or twice weekly to each student in school and watching them teach. Apart from the high cost in both time and money of this peripatetic system, it has the further disadvantage that a conflict situation is built into the relationship between supervisor and student. The former, dropping into the classroom now and then as a non-participant observer, is seen by the latter mainly in an inspectorial role as assessor and critic; and this, however good the relation between them, reduces the supervisor's efficacy in his other and more important role as helper and counsellor. In the new system—now called the *protocol method*— the supervision is based not on a visit to the classroom, but on a detailed account by the student recalling what happened in a particular work period. The supervisor and student go over this together, the aim of the former being to help the student to become aware of things he did not realize at the time, to reach his own evaluation and make suggestions for improvement. This reduces the role conflict, develops the student's capacity for self evaluation, and has the further advantage that the supervisions can take place at any time convenient to lecturer and student. Since the date of the second Leicester working party, the protocol method has been used at St. Gabriel's College, London, and Bede College, Durham, and other colleges are considering its use.[3]

The protocol method had its origins in the social work field where the obsession with assessment and examinations so prevalent in the educational field is much less in evidence. It so happens that when the substance of this chapter was given in a talk at the Westhill Conference on Youth Service and Interprofessional Studies there had just been published by the National Council of Social Service a report by Miss Joan Tash, *Supervision in Youth Work*, giving an account of a project in the training of youth leaders which used a system of supervision similar to that described above.[4]

To return to the 1966 Leicester working party, it was agreed that the national committee should remain in being, but that for the immediate future it should have as its main task the promotion of regional groups where trainers of teachers and social workers could meet to exchange their knowledge and experience, and foster any plans for joint courses that seemed feasible in their region.* The working party suggested three main tasks for the regional groups: first, to make a survey of all the experiments being carried out or attempted of an interprofessional nature; second, to make a survey of the many new kinds of appointment which lie between the boundaries of the established schemes of training, and to ascertain what these new social educational posts entail. In some cases the posts are not new (e.g. head teachers), but their functions are changing. The need was expressed for a professional reference group for

* A number of these regional study groups are now in operation and others are in process of formation. Details can be obtained from the Secretary of the National Committee, Mr. George Kitson, John Clare Building, Kettering Road, Northampton.

the purposes of identity for such workers; and third, to explore and define areas of interprofessional training with new foci. It was felt that experiment and the different orientation of courses might more easily take place in the newer universities and in technical colleges undertaking teacher training.

The 1966 Leicester working party concluded that, in general, it would be wiser to concentrate on producing better social workers and better teachers rather than to attempt to produce a hybrid with a dual qualification. But it recognized that there was much to be gained from closer association of both students and staff concerned with preparation for the different professions; the gain would come not from minimizing the differences in professional training, but rather from enlarging the field of communication between the different branches and exposing people to the challenge of the differences. The value of this has been abundantly demonstrated in the conferences and working parties described above. We need to extend these more to our students. It was also recognized that there may well be fields of work where the dual qualification would be relevant and appropriate. And one of these, surely, is the field of youth work training. Youth workers equally with teachers are fundamentally concerned with the education of young people; in so far as schools have come to rely more on evoking interest and involvement to provide motivation for learning, the two fields of work are brought closer together; and in some areas, youth wings are being incorporated in new schools, and appointments are being made which involve working in both school and centre. Leicestershire has a scheme for providing adult centres also in the same institution. We are moving slowly towards a new conception of schools as learning centres for the whole community, in which younger and older use the same facilities; to staff these centres we shall need people much less stereotyped and compartmented in their roles than is the case at present, much more flexible and interchangeable.

Already, as at Westhill and Edge Hill, youth work and teacher training are being brought into close association. It is generally recognized that the course at the National College for the Training of Youth Leaders, planned to provide emergency courses of 1 year's duration, needs to be lengthened and brought into closer association with kindred forms of interprofessional education. It is to be hoped that this can be done without losing the investment of specific skill and motivation which has been built up at the Leicester College. Rather, we would want this to be made more available to other branches of interprofessional work.

I have no doubt at all that the youth leader of the future will also be a qualified teacher with the option of transferring from one field of work to the other, or of working part-time in both. Nothing else makes sense in terms either of career prospects or of the nature of the work. And I am equally certain that both spheres of work will gain from the close association at the initial training level and also subsequently in the field, whether school or centre, and in the growing provision for in-service education, both full- and part-time. The main lesson we have to learn, and pass on to pupils and students, is that in a society with an accelerating rate of change built into its technological foundations, learning is a life-long process, not one that ceases to be necessary when one leaves school or gets a qualification. If this lesson is learnt, the distinction between teacher and student or leader and club member becomes one of degree rather than of kind.

REFERENCES

1. P. HALMOS (Ed.), *The Teaching of Personality Development to Students of Education and Social Work*, Sociological Review Monographs Nos. 1 & 2, Keele University, 1958 and 1959; P. HALMOS (Ed.), *Moral Issues in the Training of Teachers and Social Workers*, Sociological Review Monograph No. 3, Keele University, 1960; P. HALMOS (Ed.), *The Teaching of Sociology to Students of Education and Social Work*, Sociological Review Monograph No. 4, Keele University, 1961.
2. For a detailed exposition of this in the field of teacher education see J. W. TIBBLE (Ed.), *The Study of Education*, Routledge and Kegan Paul, 1966.
3. For fuller details of this experiment and its applications, see the following articles:
   I. CASPARI and S. J. EGGLESTON, A new approach to supervision of teaching practice, in *Education for Teaching*, 1965, no. 68, pp. 42–52; J. W. TIBBLE, Practical work training in the education of teachers, in *Education for Teaching*, 1966, no. 70, pp. 49–54; J. R. BAKER, "A teacher co-tutor scheme," in *Education for Teaching*, 1967, no. 73, pp. 25–30.
4. M. JOAN TASH, *Supervision in Youth Work*, N.C.S.S., 1967.

Contributors

INGA BULMAN is a graduate in social studies and a trained social caseworker. She worked as a probation officer until her present appointment as Lecturer in the Youth and Community Services Section at Westhill College of Education, where she has special responsibility for the teacher/youth leader and teacher/social worker courses. With Fred Milson she was joint organizer of the national conference which gave rise to these papers.

MAURICE CRAFT was formerly Head of the Sociology Department at Edge Hill College of Education which developed the initial and in-service training of teacher/social workers, teacher/youth leaders, careers guidance specialists, and teachers of immigrant children. Now Senior Lecturer responsible for advanced courses at Exeter University Institute of Education. Joint editor of *Linking Home and School* (1967) and *Guidance and Counselling in British Schools* (1969), and contributor to *Education and Social Work* (1967).

FRANK DAWTRY was a prison welfare officer and Secretary of the West Riding Discharged Prisoners' Aid Society. He was Secretary of the National Council for the Abolition of the Death Penalty from 1946 to 1948, and from 1948 to 1957 was General Secretary of the National Association of Probation Officers.

A. N. FAIRBAIRN was formerly Assistant Education Officer responsible for Further Education and Youth Service in Lancashire, and since 1961 has been Deputy Director of Education for Leicestershire County Council. He is a member of the Youth Service Development Council, and was Chairman of a committee of the council which studied the relationships between schools, Youth Service and further education.

HERBERT HEGINBOTHAM is organizer of the Youth Employment Service for the City of Birmingham Education Committee. He is a Fellow of the Institute of Youth Employment Officers, and is Vice-Chairman of the Youth Employment Service Training Board. He is author of *The Youth Employment Service* (1951).

D. C. MARSH carried out research at Birmingham University until the outbreak of war, and subsequently lectured in social studies at University

College, Swansea. He became Professor of Social Science at Victoria University, New Zealand, and is now Head of the Department of Applied Social Science at Nottingham University. His publications include *National Insurance and Assistance in Great Britain* (1950), *The Future of the Welfare State* (1964), and *The Changing Social Structure of England and Wales* (1965).

JOHN BARRON MAYS spent many years in education and social work as teacher, youth club leader, and settlement warden, and is now Eleanor Rathbone Professor of Social Science at Liverpool University. A specialist in criminology and community studies, his many publications include *Growing up in the City* (1954), *Education and the Urban Child* (1962), *Crime and the Social Structure* (1963), *The Young Pretenders* (1965), *The School in its Social Setting* (1967), and *School of Tomorrow* (co-author) (1968).

FRED MILSON, Principal Lecturer and Head of the Youth and Community Service Section at Westhill College of Education, is a member of the Youth Service Development Council. He was a member of the Council's subcommittee which produced the report, *Immigrants and the Youth Service* (1967), and was also Chairman of the D.E.S. Committee which studied the Youth Service and the adult community. Publications include *Social Group Method and Christian Education* (1963) and *Group Methods for Christian Leaders* (1965).

R. D. SALTER DAVIES was formerly Staff Inspector for the Youth Service at the Department of Education and Science, and is now Chief Inspector for Further Education. He was an assessor to the Ministry of Education Committee which produced the Albemarle Report (1960).

LESLEY SEWELL was General Secretary of the National Association of Youth Clubs until her retirement in 1966, and has since been connected with the Study Group on training for community work for the Gulbenkian Foundation. A member of the Central Advisory Council for Education (England) which produced the Newsom Report (1963), she is currently a member of the Youth Service Development Council and a Governor of the National College for the Training of Youth Leaders.

J. W. TIBBLE was formerly Director of the Leicester University School of Education, and is now Academic Secretary of the Universities' Council for the Education of Teachers. He was closely associated with the interprofessional conferences at Keele, Leicester and Nottingham universities (1958–61) which gave rise to the present national Interprofessional Committee of which he is Chairman. His many publications include *The Study of Education* (1967).

EILEEN YOUNGHUSBAND lectured for many years at L.S.E., and began the first generic casework course there in 1954. Was subsequently Advisor to the National Institute for Social Work Training, and Chairman of the Working

Party which produced the Younghusband Report (1959). Currently a member of the Central Training Council in Child Care, the Probation Training Committee, and the Council for Training in Social Work. Her many publications include *Social Work in Britain* (1951) and *Social Work and Social Change* (1964).

Index